I want to thank my wife Rachel who is my rock and my best friend, without her
happen

Thank you for always being there and being you!

Prince2 2017 for beginners!

PRINCE2 2017 stands for **P**rojects **In C**ontrolled **E**nvironments and is a widely used project management methodology that originated in the United Kingdom and is now in its third iteration.

I decided to write this book to support the new Project Manager or anyone interested in the art of Project Management and support the achievement of the Prince2 2017 Foundation qualification. The information contained is based upon the most recent edition of the Prince2 2017 manual.

Prince2 2017 – The Introduction!

The key to using Prince2 2017 successfully or implementing Prince2 2017 as a methodology to support the delivery of your projects, lies in understanding the elements of Prince2 2017 and how each of these elements work together

Prince2 2017 is an integrated system, whereby each of the elements can have multiple relationships throughout the project management method. The elements of Prince2 2017 interact with each other and are not horizontal or linear, they form an intricate jigsaw puzzle that when used together in the correct manner, each element supports the entire jigsaw and only when used correctly will you see the big picture in all its glory

The only piece of the methodology that is linear is the Processes, which has a clearly defined set of steps where the next stage or process cannot be started until approval to close the previous stage is received, along with approval to move forward into the next stage.

The easiest way to achieve a pass for the Prince2 2017 Foundation is to fully understand the big picture and then delve into each of the separate elements and understand them at a granular level and how they interact with each other.

What is Prince2 2017

Prince2 2017 as highlighted already stands for Projects In Controlled Environments and was first developed in 1989 by the Central Computer and Telecommunications Agency (CCTA) in the United Kingdom to implement and manage IT-based projects, the 2 denotes that it is the second iteration and the latest release is known as Prince2 2017 whereby the 2017 indicates the year of the update.

In essence or in its simplest form, Prince2 2017 is a Project Management Methodology that is designed to be generic and can be applied to any type of project, which is one of its key strengths. It lays out a specific set of processes for the Start-Up, Management and Closing of the project. These individual processes provide guidance for the Project Management Team throughout the lifecycle of the project.

So, why is Prince2 2017 so popular, in essence the answer to this comes from its ability to manage any type of project and be tailored to the specific project environment and organisation, it also separates the management products from the specialist products and successfully separates the management team from the delivery team allowing the focus on products and quality to ensure that what is delivered is fit for purpose and meets the needs of the customer\user

The Integrated Elements of Prince2 2017

Prince2 2017 starts with the 4 Integrated Elements. These elements form the basis or structure for which the project can be supported.

In its simplest form, the 4 elements are the foundation of your house, without this foundation your house will not be stable

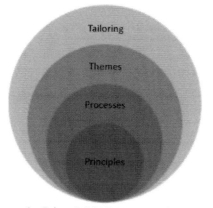

Figure 1 - Prince2 2017 Integrated Elements

Within the book, there is a chapter dedicated to each of the elements, this is aligned to the Prince2 2017 Manual and where necessary I will also refer to the Prince2 2017 Manual pages to support your learning and the revision process

It is key that you have a copy of the Prince2 2017 manual, especially if you aim to proceed to the Practitioner qualification,

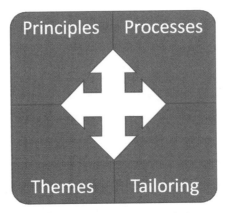

Figure 2 Prince2 2017 Integrated Elements

Prince2 2017 Principles
The Prince2 2017 Principles are a set of "best Practices" or "obligations" that **must** be followed to determine whether your project is in fact being managed as a Prince2 2017 Project, there are 7 Principles that need to be followed and these are:

1. Continued Business Justification
2. Learn from experience
3. Defined roles & responsibilities
4. Mange by Stages
5. Manage by exception
6. Focus on products
7. Tailor to suit the project

Within your Manual the principles are defined between pages 20-28

Prince2 2017 Themes
Prince2 2017 Themes, as with the principles, there are a set of 7 specific areas that are continuously and simultaneously addressed, monitored and maintained\updated throughout the lifecycle of the project

The 7 Themes are:
1. Business Case
2. Organization
3. Quality
4. Plans
5. Risk
6. Change
7. Progress

The Themes are addressed within the Prince2 2017 Manual between chapters 5-12, we will discuss each of them separately within the book

Prince2 2017 Processes

The Prince2 2017 Processes are often the simplest to understand, being linear and carried out in a defined and sequential order from starting the project to closing the project. Each of these processes has a checklist of activities, products and accountabilities and are contained within the Prince2 manual between chapters 13-20

The 7 processes are (with the Prince2 2017 abbreviations):
1. Starting Up a Project Process (SU)
2. Directing a Project Process (DP)
3. Initiating a Project Process (IP)
4. Controlling a Stage (CS)
5. Managing product Delivery (MP)
6. Managing a Stage Boundary (SB)
7. Closing a Project Process (CP)

So why do we need Projects?

For an organization in modern society to survive it must walk a very thin line between operations being consistent and available and providing change, new products, enhancements

We all remember the name Kodak, a household name that when said conjured an image pf photographs and the Kodak logo, but a failure to change and adapt meant a household name became consigned to history and a series of whitepapers explaining how and why they failed.

Embracing change, is also about embracing projects. Projects by their nature deliver or introduce change, however they aim to deliver it in a controlled manner with a view to ensuring the right projects are approved and the products delivered are fit for purpose and meet the needs of the customer

Successful organisations find ways to manage both their Business as Usual (BAU) and introduce change, using Prince2 2017 as a tool to enable the delivery change

So, what is a Project, the Prince2 2017 manual has a very clear definition of a project on page

Prince2 2017 – Definition of a Project

'A Temporary Organisation that is created for the purpose of delivering one or more business products according to an agreed business case"

There are a number of key characteristic's that differentiate projects from business-as-usual, these are:

- **Change**: Projects are the means by which organisations introduce change (new products, processes, features)
- **Temporary**: As detailed within the definition, projects are temporary, once the change has been made or implemented, the need for the project no longer exists. Projects have a clearly defined and understood lifespan. A beginning and an end that is understood. Maintenance\updates etc are not part of the project, they are classically business-as-usual or in the instance of a major product update, could be a new project in its own right
- **Cross-Functional**: Projects involve teams with different skills, or multiple people with the same skills working on different aspects of the project. Projects can span multiple departments or even multiple organisations.
- **Unique**: Every project is unique, even if you're an organisation that delivers "off the shelf products" each project is unique in that in may have different customers, team members, timelines and these variances are what makes every project unique
- **Uncertainty**: projects by their nature introduce change, and this introduces uncertainty. These will be threats and opportunities over and above those relating to business-as-usual. Projects are risky and the process of managing this risk within the context of the project is about the reduction of the probability or impact of a threat.

These characteristics allow you to understand Prince2 2017 and its definition, in essence: The Prince2 2017 project creates a temporary and cross functional team (often) within a larger organization, to deliver an agreed product to an agreed business case

The Prince2 2017 Method and why do we need it?

Prince2 2017 allows an organization to implement change without draining the resources supporting the business-as-usual processes, it provides the framework for effectively delivering projects using specialist skills, planning, delegation, process monitoring, management of specialist teams

Projects often have a number of parts \processes to deliver ,from the most basic project to the most complex often having hundreds or even thousands of parts\processes\deliverables. These are often created by specialists working as teams or independently.

A methodology like Prince2 2017 provides a control function for all of these separate parts of the project and ensures they are working together towards a common goal, and in the correct order. This ensures a cohesive product that is delivered as fit for purpose, on-time and in budget!

Another key aspect or benefit of Prince2 2017, is the management of risk, as we have already seen a project by its nature introduces change into an organization and change introduces risk. Prince2 2017 adds a layer of management in the form of Risk Management. These management methods are tried and tested and are taken from the Management of Risk Guidance created by the Office of Government Commerce. The management of risk doesn't aim to eliminate risk, that's is impossible, the aim is control risk more effectively and where possible reduce the probability of the risk occurring or impact of the risk if it does occur

What is it we wish to control?

Prince2 2017 defines the areas we wish to control as the aspects or variables, and there are 6 of them. These are common to all projects and are called the performance targets, if your project fails to meet any of them – its performance is falling short and potentially has a poor outcome! The Project Manager must constantly monitor the project against all 6 of these aspects\targets or objectives

Within the Prince2 Foundation you will see the terms, Variables, Aspects, Performance Targets interchangeably and therefore you should ensure you learn to recognise them and the link to the 6 aspects of Project Management

So, what are these 6 aspects\variables\performance targets?

- **Time**: Closely linked to costs, this is the most often asked question in relation to the project, will it be finished on time? Are we on-time? This is an area the Project Manager should focus on, the sooner any potential delays are identified, potentially the less costly they will be
- **Cost**: The project must be affordable and represent value for money. Every project has a budget and those funds are not unlimited. The Project Manager must monitor the project costs and detect possible cost over-runs as early as possible
- **Quality**: Prince2 2017 judge's quality on the products suitability for the purpose it was designed for, during the development\delivery process the Project Manager should monitor for shortfalls in quality and these should be addressed immediately
- **Scope**: This is the important one and the area that can cause the most issues with the dreaded Scope Creep! This is exactly what the project will deliver. All stakeholders involved in the project must agree to the scope to ensure there are no misunderstanding or gaps in the scope, it is also beneficial to clearly define what is not in the projects scope
- **Benefits**: The reason for the project and often the most overlooked question, why are we doing this project? The project should deliver a return upon its investment (ROI). The Project Manager must thoroughly understand this purpose and regularly re-evaluate the ROI, the Executive will constantly be asking the question is the project value for money?

- **Risk**: As we have highlighted already, projects introduce change, and this brings uncertainty. The question is how much risk as a project or organization are we prepared to accept, The Project Manager will build the strategies for managing risks based upon the stakeholder's definition of what level of risk is acceptable

What is the role of the Project Manager in Prince2 2017

The role of the Project Manager is to lead the project on a day-2-day basis as delegated by the Executive. Successful project management begins with the understanding of the projects benefits. By understanding the overall purpose and benefit of the project, the Project Manager is able to make the decisions necessary to complete the project

The primary job of the Project Manager is to plan the project, this includes all the tasks and activities needed to successfully complete the project. These are mapped out in advance in the Project Plan and in the order they will happen, Tasks that overlap or have dependencies will be noted in the Project Plan

Another key role of the Project Manager is Delegation, the Project Manager may be able to do the work of the specialist, but this is not their role. Delegation is a key skill; the Project Manager needs to delegate the tasks to the specialist team members or teams for the delivery of the projects products. This separation from the management layer is a key differentiator or hallmark of Prince2 2017

Once these tasks are assigned to the specialists and they commence work, the Project Manager must constantly monitor the results of their work paying particular attention to ensuring it matches the Project Plan and is aligned to the 6 variables all remain within the defined constraints

Another key responsibility of the Project Manager is to identify ways to reduce time and cost in relation to the Project. These 2 variables should be under constant review or monitoring by the Project Manager ensuring that any identified opportunities can be implemented

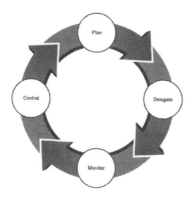

Figure 5 Project Management

What are the Benefits of using Prince2 2017?

The benefits of using the Prince2 2017 methodology are completely open, Occasionally some of those listed in the manual will appear in the exam and these are listed below:

- **Broad applicability**: Prince2 2017 is appropriate for any type of project
- **Common Language**: Prince2 2017 allows practitioners from varied environments or organizations to use the same vocabulary and methodology
- **Product Focused**: Prince2 2017 is focused on products and defines the expected outcome of the products, the quality standards that will be used to evaluate it and the roles of those assigned to review the quality ensuring products are fit for purpose
- **Ease of integration**: Organizations that use other methods to deliver projects will find that Prince2 integrates easily with methods specific to that industry

- **Clearly defined roles**: All stakeholders involved in the project know exactly what is required of them and their role within the project
- **Continuous monitoring**: Project viability is evaluated at every phase of the project process and development process
- **Management by exception**: Prince2 2017 provides a framework for escalating problems, known as "exceptions" to the next level of management when they exceed a pre-defined or agreed tolerance
- **Worldwide adoption**: Prince2 2017 is available and supported by numerous organizations and accredited training organizations

The Exam!

For your exam preparation, you will need to pay attention to:

- The 4 Integrated Elements
- The 5 characteristics of a Project
- The 6 Aspects\variables\objectives\performance targets of Project Management
- The Benefits of using Prince2

Each chapter in section 1 of the book is aligned or devoted to an Integrated Element and is aligned to the Prince2 2017 manual

Prince2 2017 Principles

The first element of Prince2 2017 is made up of the 7 Principles. These principles are a set of general best management practices that guide the implementation of the other elements.

A project must always have all 7 principles embedded and operating at all times to be classed as a Prince2 2017 project. If even 1 of the principles is not being followed, it is not a Prince2 2017 project

It is often better to think of the principles as a set of rules that must be followed, and you must conform to at all times

The principles govern the project in its entirety and are applied throughout the other 3 integrated elements of Prince2 2017. You should spend time ensuring you understand how the principles match align to practices presented within the other chapters.

Continued Business Justification

As defined in the Prince2 2017 definition of a project – "Delivered to an agreed business case" the Prince2 2017 project must have valid justifications or reasons before it can be begin, these justifications must carry on throughout the lifecycle of the project. These justifications must be documented and approved by all stakeholders

The Continued Business Justification Principle is specifically designed to ensure a project is actually worthwhile and an effective use of an organizations time, resources and money. The projects justification, purpose and ROI are evaluated before the project officially begins, this is prior to any significant resources or funds being assigned to the project

These evaluations continue throughout the project to ensure it remains a solid investment and the justifications remain valid

This ensures that all projects remain justified and stops projects taking on a momentum of their own

Prince2 2017 states that when a project is no longer justified, it should be closed. This is considered a positive step whereby a project that no longer has a justification for the use of an organizations resources, should be stopped in a controlled manner.

This principle governs and is aligned to the Business Case Theme, where the business justification is documented and approval for the project to begin is written into the Business Case document. Once approved, the Business Case is continually monitored throughout the life of the project to ensure the projects justification remains valid

Learn from Experience

Prince2 2017 requires that all project team members learn from past experience, from previous projects, previous stages etc. These lessons are documented in the lessons log that is created specifically for this purpose, this is created by the Project Manager at the start of the project.

Learning from experience is one of the first tasks undertaken by the Project Manager where they review previous lessons and create the lessons log, this learning then continuous throughout the life of the project with the goal of continually learning and improving during the life of the project and then after the completion and closure of the project, the lessons log becomes part of the organizations lessons records to support future projects

The learn from experience principle is extremely useful and especially important if the members of the project team have never worked on or been involved in a project before. According to the 5 characteristics of a project, all projects are unique and according to the 6 variables\aspects\performance targets, this uniqueness causes or produces uncertainty (risk) due to the very nature of projects introducing change, learning from experience is an important tool for supporting the management of risk within the project and enables the "unknowns" to be reduced

If a project is totally unique and never been undertaken by an organization, then the importance of the lessons learned and documenting these into the lessons log becomes even greater in order to ensure a record is left for future projects

The learning from experience principles governs several of the steps contains in the process, it commences within the Starting-Up a Project (SU) process where a review of previous lessons logs is undertaken by the Project Manager, as the project progresses, all lessons that are learned are documented

The Progress Theme and the Quality Theme are primary focuses for this documentation, however on very large projects the documentation of lessons may take place on a stage by stage basis within the Managing a Stage Boundary Process (SB), and finally the lessons log is handed over to the organization as part of the Closing a Project Process (CP)

Defined Roles & Responsibilities
Within Prince2 2017, the roles are clearly defined with the responsibilities. This method ensures that all stakeholders associated with the project know what to expect from other team members, and what is expected of them.

The method defines three primary stakeholders common to all projects. These are

- **Business**: Those who agree with or define the projects justification and purpose. They are typically senior management with the organization and primarily concerned with ensuring the project represents value for money and provides an ROI
- **Users**: Representation for those who will use the products produced by the project or benefit from them
- **Suppliers**: Provide the specialist resources (manpower, technology, materials, skills) needed to deliver the projects products to time, cost and quality and can be internal, external or a mix of both

The Defined Roles & Responsibilities Principle requires that all three roles are represented on the Project Board, although there may be many more stakeholders involved and represented upon the project

Members of the project may come from various parts of the organization, internal or external and have a wide array of backgrounds, skills, interests and priorities. This aligns to the characteristic of projects being Cross Functional and also aligns to the Organization Theme.

To be successful every project must have a clearly defined Project Management team, along with a clearly defined structure, with documented and agreed responsibilities

Manage by Stages
Prince2 2017 states that a project is planned, monitored and controlled on a stage-by-stage basis, and breaks the project into discreet, sequential sections called Management Stages, although these can also be called Delivery Stages

Each stage is planned with only as much detail as can be managed and foreseen, each stage serves as a control point where the projects status and justification can be assessed before approval for the next stage is granted by the Project Board and the current stage is closed

The Project Manager will review the Business Case and the Project Plan to ensure that the project remains on track. This review is completed and report upon prior to the decision made by the Project Board to proceed or in cases whereby the project is no longer justified, take the decision to close the prematurely project

Management by stages solves the two major issues that are often seen as part of the planning process.

The planning horizon, due to the very nature of projects and their uncertainty, the process of creating very detailed plans that cover the entire project or go into the future are likely to be unrealistic and present more problems than they solve by being created and effectively waste time and effort in there creation.

Prince2 2017 addresses this issue by using a short-term plan called a Stage Plan. The Stage Plan only covers the active management stage, or the upcoming stage that is presented for approval and contains sufficient detail to allow the Project Manager to manage and control the project on a day-2-day basis. The Project Plan is less detailed and covers the full project at a high level and includes major milestones and deliverables etc.

The second issue that could (or often does arise), is the need to provide the Project Board sufficient control over the process without becoming a burden by demanding too much time. The more stages a project has, the more control points the Project Board will have.

The stages in the project can be adjusted dependent upon the complexity, risk and importance of the project. For example, if a project is low risk and not necessarily complex, there is no reason why the management stages cannot be longer

Prince2 2017 requires that there are at least 2 management stages: one to support the initiation and at least one more stage to complete the delivery.

Manage by Exception

Prince2 2017 projects have defined limits for each of the project objectives\variables\performance targets enabling the establishment of delegated authority, these limits are called tolerances

Prince2 2017 requires that these limits are defined against the 6 variables in the form of tolerances, any variable that exceeds this defined tolerance is managed in the form of an exception, when the exception occurs it triggers an escalation to the next level of management.

Management by Exception sets very clear boundaries for accountability within the project at each management level

Issues that are within the agreed or defined tolerances can be handled by the Project Manager, ensuring that only issues that need the support or management by the Project Board are escalated and their time is not wasted

The Management by Exception Principle governs how tolerances are defined and managed for the 6 variables within the Progress Theme

Focus on Products

Prince2 2017 has a distinct emphasis on the output over the activity, which is the definition of the Focus on Products Principle.

With Prince2 2017 focusing upon the outputs rather than the activity, the end product is defined and understood at the beginning of the project. This understanding of the project products then drives and supports the project

By understanding and clearly defining the product requirements using tools like the Project Product Description (P2 A.21) and the Product Description (P2 A.17), a clear understanding of the purpose of the project, its expected use and the quality requirements and defined and agreed by the stakeholders at the beginning of the project.

The planning can then be undertaken with a clear picture of the projects output and the stakeholder's expectations in relation to the benefits (which are defined within the Business Case)

The Project Product Description and Product Description support the estimations process for time, materials, costs, work schedules etc, this also reduces the possibility of scope creep by clearly defining the projects products and boundaries of the products and the project

The Principle of Focus on Products aligns to the Plans and Quality Themes and governs how the products are specifically defined, delivered and assessed as fit for purpose

Tailor to suit the project

Contrary to popular belief, Prince2 2017 is extremely versatile and can be applied to any type or project or organisation. This is supported by the principle of Tailoring and this is what makes the methodology so versatile.

For example, if a project is small in terms of time and complexity, the whole project team works together and sees each other daily, there may not be a need for such formal reporting. The project could therefore be delivered using a series of checklists and minuted meeting's, this is perfectly acceptable in Prince2 2017 and would be documented within the Project Controls and the Project Initiation Documentation

It is also crucial to understand the benefit of tailoring Prince2 2017 based upon the project, its complexity, risk and the potential benefits. If Prince2 2017 is not tailored, the effort to deliver the project could be in-appropriate or disproportionate and could mean the project costs\time and effort are not relative to the needs of the actual project.

Prince2 2017 Themes

The Themes element identifies the 7 aspects of Prince2 2017 that are continually managed, assessed and reviewed throughout the lifecycle of a Prince2 2017 project

The 7 Themes are secondary or subordinate to the 7 principles but are above the 7 Processes. The Themes answer the questions raised by the business that arise as part of the project (why we are doing this, what will we gain, who is doing what, how much will it cost etc.)

The 7 Themes can be aligned into 3 categories, some fall into multiple categories due to the nature of the Theme itself.

The first category establishes the standards and tolerances for the Project and is aligned to the 6 Project Variables to ensure that in the event an exception arises and is evaluated against the projects continued viability. The Themes aligned to group 1 are Business Case, Quality and Plans

The second category supports the question of how the project will be measured, monitored and controlled. The Themes in this group are Quality, Risks, Change and Progress

The third category defines the roles and responsibilities and The Organization Theme is aligned to this group

The 7 Themes are integrated and are continuously carried out throughout the projects entire lifecycle. All 7 Themes must be used at all times; however, they can be tailored, and each theme has specific "minimum requirements" defined within the Prince2 manual and these should be reviewed and understood in the context of the individual project

Business Case Theme

The purpose of the Business Case Theme is to take the idea for the project, document the justification or make a case for it within the context of the organization by defining the benefits, developing the metrics for measuring those benefits and documenting them in the for of the ROI

If the benefits for the project are sufficient, the project will be approved and allowed to Start-Up, however as defined within the Principle of Continued Business Justification, if the project benefits are no longer valid and cannot deliver against the documented benefits\ROI at any point during the projects lifecycle, the project should be stopped or changed.

The Business Case Theme answers the question "why" – should we devote, resources (time, money, staff, systems, services) to this project?

The Business Case Theme requires a written document that document's the case for the overall project and includes an executive summary supported by:

1. The reasons for the project and why it is necessary
2. The options (Do nothing, Do the minimum, Do Something) A project will only proceed if its benefits\ROI outweigh the alternatives and the costs to deliver and support the project
3. The benefits that are derived from the project
4. Any potential dis-benefits
5. The project timescales (to deliver the project and commence benefits reporting)
6. The estimated project costs
7. The Project investment appraisal, which should include the ROI
8. A summary of major risks that could affect or impact the delivery of the project or achievement of the identified benefits

Prince2 2017 requires that the Business Case is defined and documented at the beginning of the project and is then maintained, reviewed and where necessary updated throughout the projects lifecycle. The Project Board formally verifies the Business Case at key control points, primarily at the end of each Management or Delivery Stage, however the Business Case should also be reviewed against potential changes or major risks when raised

The Executive has ultimate responsibility for the Business Case and the investment on behalf of the business

The Business Case Theme is divided into three parts, Outputs, Outcomes and Benefits

The project may result on one or more Outputs (the specialist products delivered by the project), those changes result in one or more Outcomes (the Outcome is the change derived from the projects specialist products delivered, because Prince2 2017 projects deliver change) and this Outcome enables the realization of the identified Benefits

Benefits Management Approach
The Business Case document is supported by the Benefits Management Approach (P2 A.1), and the Benefits associated with the project are formally defined within the Benefits Management Approach, these are reviewed at the end of each Management or Delivery Stage

The detailed Business Case cannot be completed without the benefits Management Approach, the Benefits Management Approach is created as part the Initiating a project Process and defines the plan for the realization of the benefits.

The plan includes the timings, scope, reviews that address the benefits for the project and when they will have realized

Prince2 states that benefits are "usually" realized post project, however benefits can be realized during the project and in these circumstances the Benefits Management Approach is updated to reflect that the benefits will go into Benefits Management and be reported upon.

Therefore, it is crucial that the Benefits Management Approach defines the roles and responsibilities relating to the benefits, reporting the benefits, skills needed to measure the benefits and also how those benefits will be measured and the baselines that they will be measured against

The project Manager will create the Benefits Management Approach during the Initiating a Project process (IP) and is submitted to the Project Board for review and approval. See P2 P210, Table 16.8 for the Business Case responsibilities

The project Manager will then update the Benefits Management Approach at the end of each Management or Delivery Stage to ensure it accurately reflects the project.

The Business Case and Benefits Management Approach should always reflect the most accurate information on the project in relation to time\costs and benefits

The Benefits Management Approach is the only Prince2 2017 document that lives on post project and is owned post project by the Senior User and not the Executive

Organization Theme
The purpose of the Organization theme is to document and define the roles and responsibilities of those people assigned to the project and make up the Project Management Team.

The Organization Theme answers the question of "Who" – will be responsible for each of the areas within the project, remains value for money, delivers the products required ensuring it is completed, delivers the benefits identified according to the Business Case

The Prince2 2017 Principles require that all projects have clearly Defined Roles and Responsibilities, the Organization Theme supports this principle through the representation of the three stakeholder groups: Business, User and Supplier.

The Organization theme also includes the clearly defined responsibilities for the direction, management and delivery of the project

The roles within the project are reviewed regularly during the project lifecycle to ensure they remain effective and the right resources are assigned to the project

The Organization Theme also supports the effective communication between the identified management levels and between the identified stakeholders

The Project Management Team

The Project Management Team is a temporary organization that is created with the purpose of delivering the project product to the agreed business case. It consists of three levels:

1. Project Board – provides Direction and is the top project level
2. Project Management – sits in the middle and acts as the Management level providing day-2-day management of the Project
3. Team Management – Sits at the bottom and provides the delivery\creation of the specialist products, all levels that sit below the Team Manager are considered specialists and are not included in the Prince2 2017 methodology

To ensure conflicts of interest are avoided, the Project Board and Project Management levels must be kept separate and the decision-making authority cannot be delegated

The Project Board (Business, User & Supplier)

The top level or tier of the Project Management Team is known as the Project Board, within a Prince2 2017 project provides overall direction and steers the project by ensuring it remains aligned to the agreed Business Case, remains justifiable and provides value for money

The Project board is appointed by Corporate, Programme or Customer that has triggered the project through the use of the Project Mandate

The Project Board has ultimate accountability for the success or adversely the failure of the project. It also provides a cohesive direction for the project through the Project Manager, who through the delegated authority on behalf of the Project Board manages the project on a day-2-day basis

The Project Board conducts independent monitoring of the project through its role of Project Assurance (P2 P345-346) and t is the only management group with Change Authority, although this and Project Assurance can be delegated on behalf of the Project Board

Finally, the Project Board makes sure that the Project Management Team has the necessary funding, the resources required Software, HW, Manpower etc.) to complete the project

Prince2 2017 utilises the Principle of Management by Exception, whereby the Project Manager ensures the Project Board and kept informed through the use of the Highlight Report (P2 A.11), but the Project Board only need to make decisions at the key control points within the Project Process or when an escalation occurs

To be complete and aligned to Prince2 2017, a Project Board must always include the at least one representative from each of the stakeholder interests: Business, User and Supplier

The Business representative's role is to monitor the organizations investment in the project to ensure that:

- The Business case that approved the project to be launched continues to exist throughout the projects lifecycle
- That the project provides value for money

The Executive is the formal title used within Prince2 2017 for the business representative, in your organization this may be the Project Sponsor or Senior Representative Officer

There can only be one Executive in a Prince2 2017 project, the accountabilities cannot be delegated

The User Representative is responsible for the specification of the projects outputs that are desired by the users and ensuring that the products delivered by the project fulfils them.

The Senior user is the formal title for the User Representative within Prince2 2017

The Supplier representative represents the specialist who provides the skills and resources needed to produce the specialist products. The supplier may be external, internal or can be a mix of both and in some project the suppliers can change during the project lifecycle.

The Senior Supplier is the formal title used for the representative or representation of the suppliers

Within a Prince2 2017 project there may be additional stakeholders needed or who need representation on the Project Board. Any groups or stakeholders affected by the project should be represented on the Project Board or within a Stakeholder working group within a Prince2 2017 project

The Project Board also has the responsibility for Project Assurance (P2 P345-346), mean that it monitors all areas of the project separately\independently of the monitoring practices of the Project Manager

The Project Assurance responsibilities may be delegated by the Project Board, but they must remain independent of the Project Manager, also the accountability for Project Assurance cannot be delegated only the function

The Project Board also has the authority to approve requests for changes, deviations or departures from the agreed baselines (Project specifications)

The Project Manager
The day-2-day management of the Project is the duty of the Project Manager within a Prince2 2017 project and assumes authority as delegated from the Project Board to make decisions within the agreed and documented tolerances

The Project Manager role within a Prince2 2017 project cannot be shared, there can only be one Project Manager with the management responsibility\accountability for the project

Within a Pricne2 2017 project, 5 of the 7 Processes are the responsibility of the Project Manager, apart from the appointment of the Executive within the Starting Up a Project Process and the Directing a Project Process.

The Project Manager directs the Team Managers or can assume the role of Team Manager if they have the specialist skills needed and this is agreed by the Project Board. This would normally occur in smaller projects

It is also the Project Managers job to prepare. review and update the Communication Management Approach as well as the Project Management Team Structure and this will include the preparation\creation of the role descriptions (P2 Appendix C)

Whilst the Project Manager cannot participate within the Project Assurance, they will receive feedback from the process of Project Assurance through the Project Board

The role of Project Support (P2 P347) is also part of the responsibilities of the Project Manager and whilst the formal role of Project Support is optional, the actual responsibilities are not.

Project Support can take the form of administrative tasks such as change control, risk management, financial management etc and can be delegated by the Project Manager, however overall control must be maintained by the Project Manager

The Team Manager

The role of the Team Manager is to ensure that the production of the specialist products (Outputs) is aligned to the Project Variables of Time, Cost and Quality

The Prince2 2017 methodology allows the Project Manager to act as or fulfil the role of Team Manager, however this is dependent upon the size and complexity of the project and whether the Project Manager has the requisite specialist skills needed to fulfil the role of the Team Manager

The production tasks are assigned to the Team Manager by the Project Manager in the form of Work Packages, project deliverables are clearly defined within the Work Packages including the quality requirements, quality methods, quality responsibilities, reporting requirements etc

The Team Manager is responsible for reporting to the Project Manager in the form of Checkpoint Reports and the Team Manager reports to the frequency agreed and defined within the Work Package

Within the Prince2 Manual there is no template for the Work Package as Prince2 2017 makes the assumption that the supplier will provide this based upon their own methodology

Quality Theme

The purpose of the Quality Theme is to define the quality standards, quality criteria and quality responsibilities for the products being produced, and ensuring that the products produced met the requirements in terms of quality and are essentially fit for purpose

The Quality Theme answers the question "What?" What is the purpose of the product? What does the customer expect? What are the criteria that will be used to ensure those expectations are met and ensure the product is fit for purpose? What tools or methods will be used?

The Prince2 2017 methodology maintains quality continuously throughout the projects lifecycle and the products development process. The Focus on Products Principle requires that each product is clearly defined, and all participants understand the product. The evaluation criteria in relation to the products quality during and after the development cycle has been completed are defined at the beginning of the project and refined throughout the project through the of the Project Product Description and Product Descriptions. In addition to the products quality expectations, the project itself is also subject to quality expectations and evaluations

Quality Definitions:

Prince2 2017 has borrowed some of the terms for Quality from ISO9000, however they must be clearly understood and defined within the context of Prince2 2017 to avoid any confusion

These are defined within the Glossary of the P2 Manual

Quality: A complete set of features that enable a product or process to meet expectations and satisfy needs
Scope: A list of one or more products that a project will produce, and a detailed product description for each one
Quality Management System: A complete set of standards, process and responsibilities governing the organization that been assembled to complete the project
Quality Planning: Defining all aspects of quality for a project, including the products to be delivered, product descriptions, evaluation measurements, evaluation criteria, evaluation methods, evaluation responsibilities
Quality Control: Monitoring the operations, activities, processes of those people involved within the project with the specific goal of constant improvement and recording those within the Quality Register and or the Lessons Log

Quality Assurance: The independent review of the project and the project processes, within Prince2 2017 Quality Assurance is external to the project and outside of the scope of Prince2 2017. This responsibility belongs to the Corporate, Programme or Customer. However, the caveat to this is that the Project Management Team is responsible for ensuring that the Quality Assurance Review is independently carried out

Project Assurance & Quality Assurance
Within a Prince2 2017 project Assurance and Quality Assurance are separate, although they have some overlap.

Project Assurance is the Project Boards internal process of monitoring the overall project and reporting to the stakeholders,

Quality Assurance is an external and independent review of the project to ensure it remains aligned with the required Quality Management System (Policies, Processes, Procedures)

Project Assurance is conducted independently of the Project Manager and cannot be assigned to the Project Manager, it is not conducted independently of the actual project, whilst Quality Assurance is totally independent of the project

Prince2 2017 approaches quality through its Focus on Products Principle and the alignment of this Principle to the Quality Theme. Quality is defined throughout the use of the Project Product Description and the Products Descriptions, this supports the Product Based Quality Planning technique whereby all aspects of the projects quality.

These are then formally documented within the Quality Management Approach (P2 A.22) and the Quality Register (P2 A.23). The Quality Management Approach and Quality Register are maintained throughout the projects lifecycle. The Quality Register is updated throughout the products development process ensuring that it reflects the most accurate quality information

Quality Control is the implementation and evaluation of quality from the beginning of the product's process to the completion of the products development process whereby the final approval is received

Quality Planning
Quality Planning lays the foundations for the Project Board to agree on the projects products and the quality expectations of the user community. These are then communicated to all stakeholders, again to ensure a clear understanding of the projects products and reduce the possibility of scope creep and forms the projects basis for quality control

Quality planning consists of the following 5 components:
1. **Customers Quality Expectations**: These are the broadly defined requirements for the overall project that will be the measure of project success. These are captured in a number of ways, from discussions, workshops, being clearly defined in standard's etc. and are agreed upon within the Starting up a Project Process (SU) and support the Project Product Description

2. **Acceptance Criteria**: The specific, measurable characteristics that will make a projects product acceptable to the stakeholders. Acceptance criteria are refined from the customers quality expectations, whereby they are used as a starting point and refined into actual measureable criteria that are used on the projects specialist products.

   However, during the Starting Up a Project Process (SU) the products that the project will produce may not be fully understood or defined, these can be added through the use of Product Descriptions as part of the Managing a Stage Boundary Process (SB)

3. **Project Product Description**: The Project Product Description (P2 A.21) is the definition of the overall purpose of the project and defines the products that will be delivered as part of the projects overall product. The Project Product Description includes the Customers Quality Expectations and Acceptance Criteria. It also includes the Project Level Quality Tolerances, Product Quality Tolerances.

Once approved the Project Product Description becomes part of the Project Brief and is used as part of the approval process, whereby the Project Board authorise the Initiation of the Project.

The Project product Description is a high-level document that describes the overall project and should not be confused with the specific product description for the specialist products to be delivered by the project

4. **Quality Management Approach**: The Quality Management Approach (P2 A.22) is prepared as part of the Project Initiation Documentation (PID) (P2 A.20) and is created within the Initiating a Project Process (IP) and must be approved by the Project Board, it is also reviewed by Project Assurance prior to the approval

It documents the Customers Quality Expectations, the Acceptance Criteria, Acceptance Criteria, Quality Standards, Procedures, Techniques, Tools that will be within the project in relation to quality. Where possible try and use the quality standards that are in place within the organization or programme The Quality Management Approach once approved by the Project Board is then managed under change control.

5. **Product Description**: Each product that will be delivered as part of the Prince2 2017 project should have its own approved Product Description (P2 A.17), this includes Management and Specialist Products. Each product is clearly identified, and its scope is documented within the Product Description and this should include the following:
   - **Quality Criteria & Tolerances**: The quality criteria are the specifications that must be met by the product and how they will be measured at the completion of the development\build process. Specific measurements are documented as tolerances whereby a range of acceptable measures are documented ad agreed that are then used to determine if a product is fit for purpose
   - **Quality Methods**: there are 2 types of Quality Methods within Prince2 2017, these are "In-Process" and "Appraisal" Quality planning uses the in-process quality methods, while the quality control uses both methods

     The Quality Methods section of the product description details the activities that will be used\undertaken during the development phase to review and approve the specialist product

     If specialised skills, resources or systems are needed to support this, they should be detailed within the Quality Methods

   - **Quality Responsibilities**: The Product Description details three areas of responsibility in relation to the product development,

     Producer – Representing the person\group\team responsible for the development of the product

     Reviewer(s) - Representing those who will assess the product to ensure it has met the documented requirements

     Approver(s) – The person or group who are delegated, qualified and authorized to approve the product as being complete and fit for purpose

     Typically, within a Prince2 2017 project, the Senior User will fulfil the role of review

The Quality Register
The Quality Register documents the quality events that will occur during the projects lifecycle and this is updated on a regular basis to ensure it has the most accurate and up to date information. The Quality Register serves as an audit trail in respect to quality within the project

Quality Control

Within Prince2 2017, Quality Control is the result of applying, measuring and recording the quality related activities that are documented and described within the Quality Management Approach. This includes the implementation of the Quality Methods that are defined and agreed during the Quality Planning process and any details of the Quality Reviews

Quality Methods

Within Prince2 2017 as mentioned, the quality control process uses both in-process and appraisal methods to provide inspections in relation to the products quality during the development process.

The in-process inspections should be built into the products development plan and included in the work package for the respective product. These inspections could include specialist techniques, skills or processes

Appraisal methods are undertaken upon the completion of the development process and are only carried out when the product is in its final stage, when the product can be evaluated\reviewed in its final form and assessed to confirm it meets the quality requirements and is fit for purpose. These are both accomplished through the process of testing\inspections and approvals

Quality Review technique

The Quality Review technique is recommended within a Prince2 2017 project in the absence of other processes and compliments the use of Product Descriptions (P2 P89)

There are 4 objectives of the Prince2 2017 Quality Review, these are:
- **Involve** – Ensure that key stakeholders or interested parties are involved in checking the products quality and promoting wider acceptance of the product
- **Assess** – the conformity of the product to its quality criteria
- **Baseline** – The product to ensure all changes are controlled and managed through change control
- **Confirm** – that the product is complete and meets the required quality

The Quality Review Team (P2 P90) consists of the following roles:
- **Chair** – Guides the overall process and ensures that the review is conducted properly. Chairing requires competence in facilitation and the Chair should be independent of the product being reviewed
- **Presenter** – Introduces the products and represents the producers of the product, within a Prince2 2017 project this is normally representation of the supplier.
- **Reviewer** – Responsible for the product review and represents the Senior User, confirms that the product is fit for purpose and meets the quality requirements
- **Administrator** – Provides administrative support for the Quality Review supporting the Chair and records the minutes of the Quality Review

Within Prince2 2017, in simple projects it is acceptable for roles to be combined. In those circumstances the following roles can be combined

- The Chair and Reviewer can be combined
- The Presenter and Administrator can be combined

Prince2 2017 also recommends that the Project Manager and or the Team Manager Chair Quality Review Meetings to ensure effectiveness and cohesion

Plans Theme

The Plans Theme within Prince2 2017 provides a structure for communication and control by providing the backbone by providing a series of approved plans that define and document how the products will be delivered.

Within Prince2 2017 there are three levels of planning, The Project Plan, The Stage Plan and The Team Plan. Exception Plans are only added as needed and if requested and approved replace the current Stage Plan to allow that stage to be completed

The Plans Theme answers the questions "When, Where, How, How Much, by Whom"

In Prince2 2017, the Project Plan is not a Gannt Chart, Planning within Prince2 2017 is much more comprehensive and contains much more information than just a schedule.

The plan within Prince2 enables the Project Management Team to understand:

- What products need to be delivered
- The risks (both threats and opportunities)
- Any issues in relation to the definition of scope
- Which people, specialist skills, equipment, resources are required
- When activities and events should happen and any dependencies
- Whether the targets for Time, Cost, Quality, Scope, Benefits and Risk are achievable

The plans are baselined and used for the measurement of progress

Levels of Planning within Prince2 2017

Prince2 2017's Principle of Management by Stages reflects that it not possible to plan the whole project from the outset. Planning becomes more uncertain and difficult the further into the future you try to plan.

Prince2 2017 overcomes this uncertainty by focusing the planning upon a timeframe where sufficient information is known, and the plans can be more accurately created. This is known as the Planning Horizon; future plans are created with less detail the work is closer the plan can be created with sufficient detail

The three levels of planning within Prince2 2017 make this possible by ensuring that the management needs for the scope and detail at the level of Project, Stage and Team are accommodated

Project Plan

The Project Plan provides the Project Board with the information on when a projects Time, Cost, Quality, Scope performance targets are to be achieved. It shows the major products, activities and resources required for the project to be achieved

The Project Plan is created during the Initiating a Project Process (IP) and forms part of the Business Case, it contains the Project Timelines, Costs and specifies the control points and Management Stages. The Project Plan is written by the Project Manager, supported by users and suppliers and serves as the baseline for the Project Board to measure progress during the projects lifecycle

The Project Plan should also align with Corporate. Programme or Customer as appropriate to ensure those standards are met

Stage Plan

The Stage Plan is required for each Management Stage. The Stage Plan is similar in context to the Project Plan, but each element is broken down into sufficient detail to allow for the day-2-day management of the project by the Project Manager

The Initiation Stage Plan is created during the Starting Up a Project Process (SU) and is approved as part of the Directing a Project Process (DP) to approve the Initiation Stage, all other Stage Plans are created as part of the Managing a Stage Boundary Process (SB).

The Project Manager writes the Stage Plans, using the Project Plan as the initial guide and then updates the Project Plan to reflect the updated information based upon the approved Stage Plan. Remember the Project Plan should reflect the most accurate and up to date information in relation to the project and the forecast for the next stage until that is completed

This ensures that detailed planning is completed within the planning horizon and ensures effort is not wasted trying to plan stages too far in the distant future.

Team Plans
The Teams Plans are optional within a Prince2 2017 project and the creation of the Team Plan is the responsibility of the Team Manager. The Team Plan supports the completion of the associated Work Packages during the Managing Product Delivery Process (MP)

The formality of the Team Plan will very according to the needs pf the project, if the Team Manager is an external supplier, it may be inappropriate to for the Project Manager to see that organizations internal planning process

Within Prince2 2017, there is no template for the Team Plan, again this is in context that the Team Manager is possibly from an external organization and therefore they will have their own internal processes\standards and as such forcing a secondary process\template could be counter productive

Exception Plan
The Exception Plan follows an Exception Report and for a Stage Plan exception, it covers the period from the present to the end of the current Management Stage, if the Exception is at project level, the project plan will be replaced

In the event the Exception Plan has been requested by the Project Board, the Project Manager will create the Exception Plan to allow the Stage to be completed, once approved by the Project Board the Exception Plan becomes the part of the Stage Plan it was designed to replace – effectively becoming the Stage Plan

The Project Board has the authority to approve any replacement Stage Plan, the replacement of any Project Plan may be subject to Corporate, Programme or Customer approval, dependent upon the authority granted to the Project Board

Exception Plans are not used to address tolerances relating to Work Packages, the Team Manager reports the issue to the Project Manager who will then manage this in accordance with the agreed tolerance levels for the stage

The Prince2 approach to planning
Prince2 2017 approaches planning in the context that products should be identified upfront ensuring they form the foundation for the planning activities and understanding the resources\skills needed to produce them

This is the core of Product Based Planning and guides all three levels of planning within Prince2

Step 1: The Project Product Description
The Project Product Description is started within the Starting Up a Project Process (SU) with the Outline Business Case (P2 A.2) and forms part of the Project Brief (P2 A.19)

The Project Product Description is prepared by the Project Manager and is approved by the Project Board, with a review completed\undertaken by Project Assurance (P2 P173). As the Project Product Description is created in the Starting Up a Project Process (SU), there may not be sufficient information or clear direction on what the project will produce, at this stage the Project Product Description is used to define the projects scope, requirements, customers quality expectations and acceptance criteria

The Project Product Description provides the foundation for the project and its approval to initiate as part of the Project Brief

Step 2: The Product Breakdown Structure

The plan is broken into its major products or components and is then broken further down until the appropriate level of detail for the plan is reached.

Prince2 2017 call this hierarchical representation of the project products the Product Breakdown Structure (P2 Appx D)

The process of creating the Product Breakdown Structure is undertaken as part of a team representing the different levels of the Project using workshops, brainstorming, meetings etc to ensure the most information is obtained to support the project and the creation of the Product Breakdown Structure

Step 3: Creating the Product Descriptions

Once the Product Breakdown Structure is created and a clear understanding of the Project Product and the products that are needed to create this, the Product Descriptions can be created

Each product should have its own Product Description, however in the early stages of the project, the Product Descriptions may simply be placeholders until further into the project and more information is known.

Product Descriptions can and should be refined throughout the projects lifecycle. The Project Manager will create the Product Descriptions and as with the Project Product Description, these will be created using members of the Project Team in consultation

Close attention and time should be taken in relation to the Quality Planning Process when writing the Product Descriptions

Step 4: The Product Flow Diagram

When writing both the Project Product Description and Product Descriptions, an understanding of the development\creation flow and dependencies and this information is used to create the Product Flow Diagram

Information in relation to products that are created within the project is included in the Product Flow Diagram with special note in relation to External Products

Identification of activities and dependencies

The identification of Products is not sufficient for scheduling and control within a Prince2 2017 project. The activities listed should include the management and quality checking activities as well as the activities needed to develop the specialist products.

External products that are required should be clearly defined.

Once these activities are defined, the sequence and dependencies between them (and products) should also be identified. t is key the success of the project to identify the dependencies and document them within the project plan and stage plans. This is the key purpose of the Product Flow Diagram

The definition of a dependency is any activity that is dependent upon another. There are two types of dependency

Internal Dependency - Is a den=pendency between two or more project activities, in this scenario the Project team has control over the dependency

External Dependency – is a dependency between a project activity and a non-project activity. In the case of a non-project activity that is undertaken by resources not assigned to the project, the Project team has no control over the dependency and should closely monitor it where possible, it may also be tracked as a risk within the project risk register

Preparation of Estimates

The advanced forecasting of time, effort and resources is required within Project Management. The estimation process quantifies these into facts and figures, however it should be noted that these are estimates and are rarely accurate or exact. They often need to be adjusted once more information is known about the project and the products.

The estimation of time and cost is key the management decision making process and time should be taken to ensure these are as accurate as possible

Preparation of the Schedule

The schedule (the classic MS Project Gannt Chart!) sets out the timeframe for achieving the Projects Objectives.
There are many tools that support the creation of the Project Schedule, MS Project is the most prolific and widely used.

Preparing the schedule has several steps within a Prince2 Project

Step 1: Define the sequence of activities

Having identified the activities and their dependencies and estimated their duration and effort. The next task is to determine the most optimum sequence in which they should occur to achieve the Project Objectives

This is an iterative task as the assignment of resources may affect the actual estimated effort and the duration of a stage or project

It is crucial that the sequencing is undertaken with support from Subject Matter Experts to ensure they are in the correct order and the overlaps are built in as needed to support the sequence and development process

Step 2: Resource availability

Resources assigned to the project are not just human, material resources should be included and quantified, and the availability assessed

The criticality of the resources can affect the cost and time in relation to the project, a resource that is critical and with limited availability, it may necessary to purchase additional resources

Step 3: Resource Assignment

Resources should be matched to the activities, at this point in the process, the project schedule should have sufficient information to allow the assignment of resources and the assignment should always be in full agreement of the person or resource owner

Step 4: Resource Levelling

After the assignment of resources, it may mean that the usage is uneven and some of those assigned are over utilised. It may be necessary to re-arrange those resource assignments

This is the levelling of resources, this is easiest to achieve using a tool like MS Project

Step 5: Control Points

The draft schedule enables or defines control points that will need to be confirmed or agreed by the Project Board.

These control points are points within the schedule where an approval or decision is needed from the Project Board. These typically occur Stage Boundaries and are often aligned to major deliverables, contract points or payment milestones

When planning these control points, sufficient time should be given to ensure that the Project Board has time to review, ask questions and provide approval

Step 6: Defining Milestones

Within a Prince2 2017 project, a milestone is a key activity or event within the schedule that marks completion of an activity. This could be a Work Package, Contract Signature etc.

These milestones also provide a way to monitor the progress of the project and assessing if it is proceeding upon schedule and to plan

Step 7: Calculating the total resource requirements and costs

The assignment of resources to the project (Human and specialist) should be collated and totalled to provide a project cost estimate which will then be included in the project budget.

This budget should include the management costs and tolerances as a separate line to ensure they are separated and the true cost of the project can be estimated

Step 8: Analyse Risks

The analysis and documentation of risks runs concurrently throughout the projects lifecycle and within the steps of the planning process

The documentation of these risks can influence the plan and the control points within the plan

Risks should be identified and documented within the Risk Register (P2 A.25)

Step 9: Document and present the plan

Once the schedule has been documented and approved, the resources assigned and their line managers\owners. It should have a narrative attached to explain the overall plan, any constraints, dependencies or assumptions made or identified within the planning process

The result of the process is a complete plan with the major milestones and an understanding of Time and Cost

A summary version of the plan should be created for the purposes of providing information to ensure the Project Board and stakeholders have the right level of information

Risk Theme

The very nature of a project is to introduce change, and therefore by their nature, projects introduce and involve risk

The purpose of the Risk Theme is to identify, assess and control uncertainty (risk) with the project

The Prince2 2017 Risk Theme answers the question of "what if" - What if a deliverable is late, what if the materials are delayed? what if a Supplier fails to deliver?

The management of risk is an activity that is continuous activity that occurs throughout the lifecycle of the project. It supports the Continuous Business Justification Principle by providing the Project Board with confidence and clarity that the project will meet the objectives defined and remains worthwhile, value for money and should continue

The Prince2 Approach to Risk

The Prince2 definition of risk is (P2 P120)

"An uncertain event or set of events that, should it occur, will have an effect on the achievement of objectives. A risk is measured by a combination of the probability of a perceived threat or opportunity occurring, and the magnitude of its impact on objectives "

There are 2 types of risk within a Prince2 2017 Project:

- **Threat**: A threat is an uncertain event that would have a negative impact upon objectives

- **Opportunity**: An uncertain event that would have a positive impact upon objectives

Both types of risk create type of uncertainty, both are considered risks within a Prince2 2017 project

The impact of risks will be upon the projects objectives if that risk occurs, in particular the six variables of Time, Cost, Scope Quality, Risk and Benefits

Risk Management
Prince2 2017 responds to risk using a systematic approach with a set of procedures that support the identification and assessment of risks, followed by planning and implementing the response to the identified risks.

Risk management should also include and document the project risk tolerances, risk appetite and risk profile definitions. These are all contained within the Risk Management Approach (P2 A.24) which is created during the Initiating a Project Process (IP) and forms part of the Project Initiation Documentation (PID) (P2 A.20)

Risk management within Prince2 2017 has 5 parts

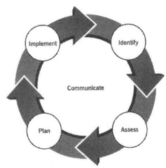

Figure 8 Prince2 2017 Risk Management Procedure

Step 1: Identify
The risks are identified and Prince2 2017 uses the Cause, Event, Effect to provide a clear and unambiguous expression of the risk

Cause: Should describe the source of the risk – the event or situation that has given rise to the risk, this is often not the actual risk but the driver that has caused the risk. These can be internal or external
Event: This should describe the area of uncertainty in terms of the threat or opportunity
Effect: Is the description of the impact or impacts that the risk would have upon the project objectives should the risk materialise

An example of a risk using the cause, event and effect is below

Cause - If the rain continues throughout the weekend
Event – The river could burst its banks
Effect – The farmer will lose the crops in the fields and result in lost revenues

The identification of risks can and will occur at any point throughout the project lifecycle, this can be done in a number of ways, using previous lessons, risk checklists, risk breakdown structure, brainstorming etc.

Step 2: Assess

The next step is to assess the risk and its impact, Prince2 2017 recommends assessing:

Probability: The probability of the threat\opportunity occurring

Impact: in relation to the project objectives at risk – for example if it will impact the cost objective, the impact of the risk should be measured in units of cost

The risk should also be assessed upon:

The impact of the risk upon the Project Plan, Stage Plan and the Business Case
The risk proximity – when is the risk likely to materialize, these ratings should again be included within the Risk Management Approach. For example, within project, within stage, 2 weeks, 4 weeks, within Work Package

These can then be presented graphically and Prince2 2017 recommends the use of the Risk Probability and Impact Grid (P2 P128 Figure 10.3)

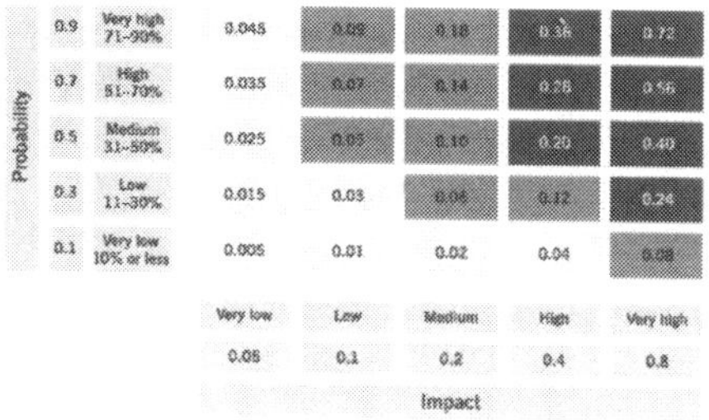

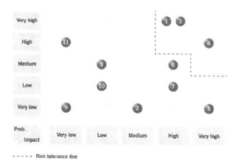

Figure 9 Prince2 2017 Probability\Impact Grid

Another useful presentation method once the risks are identified and assessed is to use a risk profile, where the risk tolerance line is highlighted and any risks that are above this line should be either raised to the Project Board or require increased management and monitoring

The Summary Risk Profile can also be used to demonstrate trends, where risk have increased in their probability or impact or have reduced

Figure 10 Prince2 2017 Summary Risk Profile

Step 3: Plan

The plan step involves identifying and evaluating the appropriate risk response to remove or reduce the threat and to maximize the opportunity

If a threat is reduced rather than being removed – the reaming threat is called the residual risk (P2 P132), in the event the residual risk is significant, it may be appropriate select multiple responses

It should also be noted, implementing the response to risk may actually lead a new risk being created, which is known as the secondary risk (P2 P133), it is essential to the project's success that these are identified and controlled in the same way as the initially identified risk

Within Prince2 there are pre-defined risk responses (P2 P134)

Avoid a threat Exploit an opportunity	This option is about making the uncertain situation certain by removing the risk. This can often be achieved by removing the cause of a threat, or by implementing the cause of an opportunity. This option may be adopted for no extra cost by changing the way the work is planned. More often though, costs will be incurred in order to remove all **residual risk** for threats and opportunities. Where costs are incurred these must be justified (i.e. the cost of response is warranted to make the situation certain).
Reduce a threat **Enhance an opportunity**	This option involves definite action now to change the probability and/or the impact of the risk. The term 'mitigate' is relevant when discussing reduction of a threat (i.e. making the threat less likely to occur and/ or reducing the impact if it did). Enhancing an opportunity is the reverse process (i.e. making the opportunity more likely to occur and/or increasing the impact if it did). Again, because this option commits the organization to costs for reduction/ enhancement now, response costs must be justified in terms of the change to residual risk.
Transfer the risk (threat or opportunity)	Transfer is an option that aims to pass part of the risk to a third party. Insurance is the classic form of transfer, where the insurer picks up the risk cost, but where the insured retains the impact on other objectives (e.g. time delay). Transfer can apply to opportunities, where a third party gains a cost benefit, but the primary risk taker gains another benefit, but this is not a commonly used option whereas transfer of threats is commonly used. Once again, the cost of transference must be justified in terms of the change to residual risk; is the premium to be paid worth it? It is important to note that some elements of risk cannot be transferred, although an organization may choose to delegate the management of the risks to a third party.
Share the risk (threat or opportunity)	Share is an option that is different in nature from the transfer response. It seeks multiple parties, typically within a supply chain, to share the risk on a pain/gain share basis. Rarely can risks be entirely shared in this way (for example, the primary risk taker will always need to protect its brand and reputation), but this can be a successful way of encouraging collaboration on risk management activities, particularly in programmes and projects.
Accept the risk (threat or opportunity)	The accept option means that the organization 'takes the chance' that the risk will occur, with its full impact if it did. There is no change to residual risk with the accept option, but neither are any costs incurred now to manage the risk, or to prepare to manage the risk in future. An example would be the risk to profitability as a result of currency fluctuations. An organization may decide to take the chance and not engage in any hedging or other provision to protect margins from wide variation in rates. This option would not be appropriate if the risk exposure exceeded the risk tolerance threshold for the organizational activity in question. Note that in a case such as currency fluctuations where the impact could be positive or negative, this is actually two risks, because a risk is the relationship between the uncertain event and the impact of that event. There is a risk leading to loss and a risk leading to gain. Framing the uncertainty as two risks allows for different responses to each part.
Prepare contingent plans (threat or opportunity)	This option involves preparing plans now, but not taking action now. Most usually associated with the accept option, preparing contingent plans in this instance is saying: 'We will accept the risk for now, but we'll make a plan for what we'll do if the situation changes.' This option applies equally to other responses and is often referred to as a 'fallback' plan (i.e. what we will do if the original response does not work). Fallback plans apply to all other strategies, even avoiding a threat and exploiting an opportunity, because the plan to avoid/exploit may not be successful despite good intentions. This option is important because it incorporates future managerial flexibility for a committed cost that is smaller than investing in more proactive strategies. This does not mean that investing now to respond to a risk is wrong, but such investments do need to be cost-justified as previously mentioned.

Figure 11 Prince2 2017 Risk Responses

Implement

The implement step, aims to ensure the selected response(s) are carried out if a risk occurs. The assignment of the roles and responsibilities is key this step, the two key roles within the implementation are:

Risk Owner: This individual is responsible for the management of the specific risk and implementing the responses

Risk Actionee: The individual supports and takes direction from the risk owner and completed the risk responses

The Risk Owner and Risk Actionee can in most cases be the same person (and often are), however when assigning these roles, the impact of assigning too many risks to a single individual should be understood and monitored. The allocation of too many risks to a single person can be counterproductive and should be avoided

Step 5: Communicate

Unlike the previous 4 steps, the communication should be continual throughout the project lifecycle and the life of the identified risks.

This step ensures that information relating to risks (threats and opportunities) within the project are communicated both internally within the project and externally to stakeholders

Risks are communicated as part of the following management products

- Checkpoint Reports
- Highlight Reports
- End Stage Reports
- End Project Reports
- Exception Reports

Care should always be taken when communicating risk to external stakeholders where the context could be misinterpreted or misunderstood

Risk Register

Within a Prince2 2017 Project, the Risk Register exists to act a repository of information for all risks identified (threats and opportunities) in relation to the project

The Risk Register is maintained by Project Support on behalf of the Project Manager however in the event there is no Project Support within the Project Management Team. The Project Manager will maintain the Risk Register

The Risk Register logs all information relating to the risks, for example the following headings are recommended within Prince2 2017 (P2 A25)

- Risk Identifier
- Risk Author
- Date raised\registered
- Risk Category
- Risk Description (Cause, Event, Effect)
- Probability\Impact\Proximity
- Risk Response
- Risk Status
- Risk Owner
- Risk Actionee

The ownership and process of maintaining the Risk Register along with the definitions of Proximity, Impact etc are contained within the Risk Management Approach

Risk Budget
In some projects it may be appropriate to identify and ring-fence an explicit portion of the projects budget to fund or manage the specific risk responses.

Although the risk budget is part of the overall project budget, it should not be used for anything other than funding the specific risk responses, it is an optional budget, and in the event, it is unused, or funds remain, Prince2 2017 states they should be returned to Corporate, Programme or Customer at the completion of the project

Change
The Change Theme enables the control of issues and change within a Prince2 2017 project. Its goal is to identify, assess and control any potential changes to the baselined aspects of the project.

The Change Theme answers the question "What is the impact?"

The Change Theme does not prevent changes, it ensures that no change is allowed to proceed or take place until the individual or individuals within the Project Management Team with the delegated authority approve the change.

This is in essence where Prince2 2017 states – is subject to change control

The Prince2 approach to change
Within Prince2 2017, all changes are identified as "issues" and the term is used to cover any relevant event that has happened, was not planned and requires management actions

Where a Risk is an event that could occur, an Issue is an event that has occurred and needs management action or control

As with risks, issues can be raised by anyone at any point in time during the projects lifecycle and by anyone with an interest in the projects outcome

There are three types of change within Prince2 2017, these are:

Request for Change	A proposed change to an agreed baseline
Off-Specification	Something that should be provided by the project but is not (or forecasted not to be) This may be a missing product or a product not meeting the agreed specifications This could also be an improvement to a specification, but this is not the agreed specification
Problem or Concern	Any other issues that requires management control or escalation by the Project Manager

Figure 12 Types of Issue

Change control is primarily twofold within a Prince2 2017 project

Issue and Change Control: The control of all issues and changes involving the projects agreed baselines, these Issues and Change Requests must be identified, assessed and either approved, rejected or deferred

Configuration Management: This activity controls the projects product configurations during the production, development, delivery and deployment into production to ensure it meets the users'\customers' needs and conforms to the agreed product baselines. Configuration Management applies to all configuration items within the project, these may be:
- Components of a product
- A product is its own right
- A release – a set of products that are managed, tested and deployed as a single unit

There are a number of key definitions within the Change Theme of Prince2 2017:

Baseline: The reference levels against which an product (management or specialist) is monitored and controlled
Configuration Item Record: A record that describes the status, version and variant of a configuration item, and any details of important relationships between them
Product Status Account: A report on the status of products. The required products can be specified by identifier or the part of the project in which they were developed

Establishing project controls

During the Initiating a Project Process (IP), the controls are established for the management of issues, changes and the configuration management

There are a number of Management Products to support the Project Controls and are created within either Starting Up a Project Process (SU) or Initiating a Project Process (IP)

- Change Control Approach (P2 A.3)
- Configuration Item Records (P2 A.6)
- Product Status Account (P2 A.18)
- Daily Log
- Issue Register (P2 A.12)
- Issue Report (P2 A.13)

Each of these documents supports the Change Theme

Change Control Approach:
is used primarily to identify, assess and control any potential change and or approved changes to the project baselines. The Change Management Approach describes the procedures, techniques and standards that will be applied and the responsibilities for achieving an effective issue management and change control procedure

The Change Control Approach should contain (as a minimum according to Prince2 2017)
- Issue Management and Change Control Procedure
- Tools and Techniques
- Record (the composition and format of the Issue Register)
- Reporting (the composition, format, recipients)
- Timings – in relation to the issue and change management activities
- Roles & Responsibilities
- Scales for priority and severity

Part of the Change Control Approach that is agreed upon between the Project Board and the Project Manager and includes the procedure for the prioritization and handling of issues as they occur during the projects lifecycle

Prince2 2017 recommends the MOSCOW technique for the prioritization, The MOSCOW technique stands for:

M – Must Have

o

S – Should Have
C – Could Have

o

W – Won't have or Would be nice to have

Other parts of the Change Control Approach are optional, and these are:

Change Authority: The Project Board has the option of delegating its decision-making powers to accept or reject requests for changes and off-specifications, this is particularly important in projects where a high number of changes is anticipated

Prince2 2017 defines this group as the Change Authority, it may include the Project manager or the group with Project Assurance responsibilities as appropriate

Whilst delegating the role of Change Authority is optional, the role is not and this is a minimum requirement for the Change Theme that the Change Authority is defined

Change Budget: As with the Risk Budget, the Change Budget is optional and set aside from the project budget to cover the costs of any requests for change, it may also include the cost for analysing those change requests. This change budget should be documented in the project plan and project controls

Configuration Item Records
The system of project controls, documents the information about each configuration item's status, version, variant and status in development. The record also lists the details of relationships between configuration items within the project

Product Status Accounts
The Product Status Account is used to provide information about the state of products within defined set of limits, these limits can vary during the development cycle, stages or the entire project.

The Project Manager can use the Product Status Account to track the development process or track the version numbers of a set of products within the project

Daily Log
The Daily Log is the informal project control used by the project Manager, it can be used at any point in the project by the Project Manager and the option is always available to start the management process informally and then transfer to the relevant Register or Log for management or escalation to the Project Board

The Daily Log also acts as an informal diary for the Project Manager and is closed at the end of the project

Issue Register
The Issue Register is a record of all information in relation to active or closed issues. It is the responsibility of the Project Manager to monitor and maintain the Issue Register

Issue Report
The Issue Report documents a single report containing the description, impact assessment and recommendations for a single request for change or problem or concern. It is only created for the issues that need to be formally managed

The report is initially created when capturing the issue and updated both after the issue has been examined and when proposals are identified for issue resolution. The issue report is later amended further in order to record what option was decided upon, and finally updated when the implementation has been verified and the issue is closed

Effective Change Control
The primary starting point for all projects is to identify whether there are any Corporate, Programme or Customer policies or process that should be applied, these are then incorporated into the projects Change Control Approach.

The process of Issue and Change Control within a Prince2 2017 project is clearly defined and supports a control process to ensure the effective management of Issues and Change

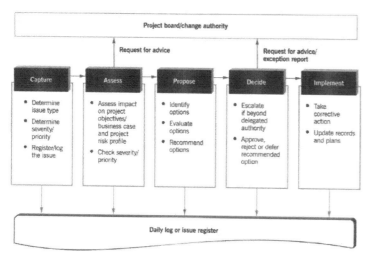

Figure 13 Prince2 2017 Issue and Change Control Procedure

Step 1: Capture

The first step in the procedure is to capture the issue and undertake analysis to determine the type of issue that been raised and whether it should be formally or informally managed, this is an initial assessment undertaken by the Project Manager where the issues severity and priority are assessed

The purpose of identifying which issues can or should be managed formally or informally is to:
- Ensure the decisions are made at an appropriate level within the Project Management Team
- Avoid the Project Board being inundated with issues and therefore diluting the time available to support the project and deal with key issues
- Reduce the administrative burden on the project when dealing with the day-2-day issues that may arise

Step 2: Asses

The next step is undertaken an assessment of the issue by performing the impact analysis. This examines the impact of the issue and whether it is worthwhile undertaking a detailed analysis of the issue, the effort including the time may cause a deviation from the project plan, therefore the Project Manager must make an initial assessment supported by Subject Matter Experts, this should consider the following:

- The Project performance Targets – Time, Cost, Scope, Quality, Benefits and Risk. This should also include whether there are any other products within the projects scope that could be affected by the issue
- The Business Case with a key focus upon the projected benefits and ROI
- Any other dependent products produced by the project
- The project risk profile, the impact of the overall risk exposure of the project

If the project is part of a programme, the impact of the change upon the programme should be considered. There may also be impacts on other projects that are not part of the programme

The impact analysis must take place and cover all three areas of the business, user and supplier, upon completion of the analysis, the severity and priority should be re-evaluated

Step 3: Proposing corrective actions

After completing a full assessment of the impact of the issue has been completed. The next step is to consider alternative options for responding to it and proposing the course of action to be undertaken

Care and attention should be given when understanding and recommending the corrective actions, if any of those identified take the stage beyond the agreed tolerances, the Project Manager should seek advice from the Project Board, the Project Manager should progress and execute the decision undertaken by the Project Board

Step 4: Deciding on corrective actions

The project manager may be able to resolve issues without the need to escalate them to the project board. For example, a minor change to an approved detailed design document that does not affect any other products could be handled by the project manager (if allowed in the change control approach), as long as it is formally recorded.

Other issues may need to be escalated to the project board (or its delegated change authority) for a decision

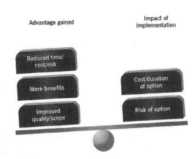

Figure 14 Prince2 2017 Options Analysis

Step 5: Implement corrective actions

The Project Manager will either:

- take the necessary corrective action, which might include updating affected products, work packages, plans and **registers,** or
- create an exception plan for approval by the project board. In both cases, the project manager will update the issue register with the decision and inform all interested parties.

Implementation of the corrective action must ensure that baselined products are updated in a controlled manner and with appropriate authorizations. If a product that has been baselined is to be changed, a new version should be created to accommodate the change and the baseline version is kept unchanged. Old baseline versions should be archived where possible, not discarded.

After an issue has been closed, the project manager should update the issue register with all of the relevant information and the date closed.

Progress

The purpose of the progress theme is to establish mechanisms to monitor and compare actual achievements against those planned, provide a forecast for the project objectives and the project's continued viability, and control any unacceptable deviations.

The Progress Theme focuses on the control and monitoring of the project to support the assessment and decision-making process. These controls are carried out at every management level of the Project Management Team, as well as by the Corporate, Programme or Customer management teams

The Prince2 2017 approach to progress

The Progress Theme supports the measurement of objectives contained within the plan and provides a mechanism to establish if they are actually being achieved. Progress is monitored at Project, Stage and work Package level within a Prince2 2017 project

Within a Prince2 2017 project, Progress Controls consist of measuring actual progress when compared against the 6 project variables (Objectives or Performance Targets) This information is used by the Project Management Team and supports the decision-making process and deciding which actions need to be taken

Prince2 2017 requires that all progress controls are documented within the Project Initiation Documentation (PID), there are three types of control

- Delegation pf management authority to the management level immediately below
- Dividing the project into Management Stages and authorizing each stage separately
- Progress reporting, both time and event driven

Of PRINCE2 2017's seven principles, the principle of Manage by Exception is particularly important to the progress theme.

Exception: An exception is a situation where it can be forecast that there will be a deviation beyond agreed tolerance levels.

Tolerances: Tolerances are the permissible deviation above and below a plan's target for cost and time without escalating the deviation to the next level of management.

There may also be tolerance levels for quality, scope, benefits and risk.

Delegation of Authority

The Manage by Exception Principle is crucial to the success of a Prince2 2017 project and the control of project progress.

Tolerances are set for each of the six project variables at the project level, also at the stage level.

The responsibility to maintain the tolerances is divided and delegated to each of the four levels within the Project Management Team.

The term exception is used to define any deviation from a tolerance that requires escalation to the next management level

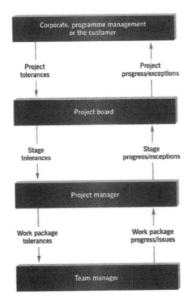

Figure 15 Prince2 2017 Tolerance Delegation & Management Layers

Within Prince2 2017, there are 4 levels of management:

Level 1: Corporate, Programme or Customer
Although not officially art of the Project Management Team within a Prince2 2017 project, Corp. Progr or Customer is the highest level of management and sets the tolerances for the overall project, these are documented as Project Level Tolerances, and are then delegated to the Project Board

If a deviation from a project level tolerance is forecasted by anyone within the Project Management Team, it will be documented and escalated by the Project Board to Corp, Prog or Customer for review and direction.

Level 2: Project Board
The next level of management is the Project Board, who have overall control of the project with the proviso it remains within the project tolerances. The Project Board agrees the tolerances for each Management Stage and then delegates these to the Project Manager (supporting the Principle of Manage by Exception).

The Project Board is responsible for reviewing project progress and the authorization for the project to continue, change or stop.

The following management products assist the project manager in establishing baselines for progress control:

- Project Plan: Includes the project-level performance targets and tolerances. Threats to the project-level tolerances need to be escalated to the project board, which will seek advice from corporate, programme management or the customer for corrective action.
- Stage Plan: Forms the basis of the day-to-day control of the management stage and detail stage-level tolerances.
- Exception Plan: May be requested by the project board after considering an exception report during the directing a project process.
- Work Package: Forms an agreement between the project manager and team manager as to the work to be completed within defined tolerances.

Appendix A A.16 and A.26 provides product descriptions for the products listed above to support the project

Level 3: Project Manager

The next level is the Project Manager, who is given overall responsibility for the project on a day-2-day basis and maintains the stage level tolerances set by the Project Board. The Project Manager is responsible for the escalation of any forecasted deviations from the stage tolerances.

The Project Manager has a number of project controls to support this, these include the Checkpoint Reports from the Team Manager, Project Plans, Stage Plans and the use of the registers\logs

Level 4: Team Manager

The final level is that of the Team Manager, who is the controller of the Work Packages and the creation\development of the specialist products within the project ensuring they remain within the agreed tolerances.

In the event a Work Package tolerance is forecasted to be exceeded, the Team Manager must raise this as an issue to the Project Manager

Types of Control

Prince2 2017 provides two types of progress control throughout the life of a project:

Event Driven Controls: These take place when a specific event occurs. This could be, for example, the end stage assessment at the end of a management stage, the completion of the PID or the creation of an exception report. It could also include organizational events that might affect the project, such as the end of the financial year.

Time Driven Controls: These take place at predefined periodic intervals. This could be, for example, producing monthly highlight reports for the project board or weekly checkpoint reports showing the progress of a work package.

Monitoring and reporting requires a time-based approach, whereas control (decision-making) is an event- based activity.

Management Stages

Prince2 2017 projects are divided into Management Stages. The activities within each of these stages are managed as a single unit with a management control point at the end of each unit\stage

The Project Board delegates the management of this section of the project to the Project Manager. The Project Manager has the authority to take corrective action as needed to ensure the stage remains within the agreed tolerances

Management Stages support the Principle of Management by Stages, The Project Board will only authorize a single stage to be active at any point. The Stages are authorized during the Management a Stage Boundary (SB) by the Project Board who will authorize the closure of the current stage and the approval for the next Management Stage to begin

The Project Manager will create the End Stage Report and the Next Stage Plan to allow the Project Board to assess the success of the current stage and authorise the next stage, this information allows the Project Board to make an informed decision and also evaluate the projects continued business justification

The number of management sages is unique to every project, however Pricne2 2017 requires that there is a minimum of 2 management stages, initiating a Project IP to establish the Project Initiation Documentation (PID) and at least one management stage.

When defining the management stages, consideration for the following should be considered by the Project Manager:
- The planning horizon
- Key decision or control points
- Risk – how much risk the project contains

The length of the stages is not defined within Prince2 2017, when considering the length of a management stage consideration should be given to:
- Longer stages mean less control points
- Shorter stages mean more control, but an administrative and time burden on the Project Board and Project Manager
- The level of complexity, risk or experience

Stages at the beginning of the project are often shorter than the middle stages, this is where the risk is lowest, and stages are often longer when risk is lower as less Project Board control is needed

Technical stages are specialist stages where the projects products are created, whilst there can only be one management stages active at any point within the project, there can be multiple technical stages and technical stages can span management stages

Technical stages often categorise the work being undertaken according to the techniques being used, for example in a construction project they could be categorised as, Design, Build, Installation, Fit-out, Handover whereas a software project could be, Requirements definition, Proof of concept, Design, Developments, Testing, Final Finish, Handover, Post Warranty Support.

Management stages are authority stages whereby the Project Board grants authority to deliver\spend, accept or commit resources in support of the management stage

Reviewing and Reporting Progress
As part of controlling a stage, the project manager will regularly review the progress of work through checkpoint reports from the Team Manager and maintain the project registers and logs.

The project manager will use this information to update the stage plan with actual progress achieved. The format and frequency of checkpoint reporting will depend on the needs of individual work packages.

The use of the registers allows the Project Manager to assess trends, for example a project may seem to be progressing well however the number of small issues being raised in that stage is increasing as it progresses, and this could be a cause for concern and require additional management controls

The following management products assist in reviewing progress:
- **Issue Register**: Contains details of all formal issues raised during the project.
- **Product Status Account**: Provides a snapshot of the status of products within the project, management stage or a particular area of the project.
- **Quality Register**: Records all planned and implemented quality activities.
- **Risk Register**: Records identified risks

In addition to these, the Project Manager will use the Daily Log for recording actions that do not require formal management or escalation.

Reporting Progress
The frequency of reporting should reflect the level of control required, and this is likely to vary during the lifecycle project and will also be unique to each project.

Prince2 2017 uses the following example, if the team is highly experienced then less frequent reporting may be appropriate, whereas for an inexperienced team the project manager may wish to increase the frequency of reporting until sufficient confidence has been gained on the capability of the team.

To support this, the following Management Products are used for reporting progress
- **Checkpoint Report**: Provides the project manager with details of progress against the work package and is typically produced by the team manager.
- **Highlight Report**: Provides the project board with details of progress for the whole project and/or management stage. The project manager produces this report.
- **End Stage Report**: Provides the project board with details of progress towards the end of each management stage (except the final stage), including information on the progress to date, the overall project situation and (together with the next stage plan) sufficient information to ask for a project board decision on what to do next with the project. The report is produced by the project manager.
- **End Project Report**: Provides the project board with information needed to evaluate the project and authorize closure. It is produced by the project manager towards the end of the project.

Appendix A A.4, A.8, A.9 and A.11 provide product descriptions for all of the above

Capturing and reporting lessons
The lessons log is used for capturing and reporting lessons when reviewing progress.

The principles of Learning from Experience ensure that the project management team learns from experience, which means that lessons are sought, recorded and actioned throughout the project lifecycle.

It is often in the reviewing of progress that lessons are identified. Lessons could include information about management or specialist processes, products, techniques or procedures that either made a contribution to the project's achievements or caused a problem.

Examples might include the performance of the project management team, the success of tailoring PRINCE2 to the project, or the analysis of quality statistics and measurements. Larger projects are more likely to make use of a lessons report as part of this process, where more detail would be helpful.

Raising Exceptions
The output from reviewing progress is a decision as to whether the work package, stage plan or project plan remain, or are forecast to remain, within agreed tolerances. Within Prince2 2017 – any forecast to exceed a tolerance is a factual statement that it will be exceeded and not a forecast that it could happen

There are three levels of exception when escalating tolerances within Prince2 2017:
- **Work Package Level Exceptions**: Having agreed work package tolerances with the team manager, the project manager should be kept informed of progress through regular checkpoint reports. If a work package is forecast to exceed its tolerances, the team manager should inform the project manager by raising an issue. The project manager will advise of any corrective actions required.

- **Stage Level Exceptions**: If the stage is forecast to exceed its tolerances, the project manager should produce an issue report to capture and analyse the details of the deviation and then provide an exception report for the project board. Based on information in this report, the project board may request that the project manager produces an exception plan to replace the plan that was forecast to exceed tolerance. The project board may also remove the cause, accept and adjust tolerance, or request more time to consider or reject the recommendations. If an exception plan is requested, the project board will conduct an **exception assessment,** similar to the end stage assessment, to review and approve the exception plan.

- **Project Level Exceptions**: If the forecast is for project tolerances to be exceeded, the project board no longer has the authority to direct the project and must refer the matter to corporate, programme management or the customer for a decision. The project board may request the project manager to produce an exception plan for the project.

The 7 Processes

The 7 Prince2 2017 Process identifies the sequential steps in the project management process that are completed to direct, manage and deliver the project. The 7 Processes are subordinate to both the Principles and the Themes.

Unlike the 7 Themes, that are carried out at all times during the project, the processes are sequential, and the end of each process is the trigger to commence the next one

The 7 Processes are:
- Starting Up a Project Process (SU)
- Directing a Project Process (DP)
- Initiating a Project Process (IP)
- Managing a Stage Boundary (SB)
- Controlling a Stage (CS)
- Managing Product Delivery (MP)
- Closing a Project Process (CP)

Starting Up a project Process (SU)

The purpose of the Starting Up a Project process which is abbreviated to SU is to conduct the pre-project activities that are necessary to lay the foundations and ensure the pre-requisites for initiating the project and satisfy Corporate, Programme or Customer that the project should go forward

The key question that SU is answering is "Do we have a viable and worthwhile project?" At this point in the projects lifecycle, the details in relation to the project may be broad and general in nature

The goal of the SU process is to do the minimum necessary to decide whether the Initiation of the project is worthwhile, the activities within the SU process are the appointment of the Project Executive and Project manager, capturing previous lessons, selecting the Project Management Team and agreeing the roles & responsibilities, preparation of the Outline Business Case assembly of the Project Brief and planning the Initiation Stage

The trigger for the SU process is the Project Mandate, which is received from Corp, Programme or Customer. The mandate contains the information that triggers the project, this could be an RFP or a feasibility study.

The Project Mandate will be refined into the Project Brief. The Project Brief should contain enough information to make the decision to initiate the project.

Corp, Programme or Customer will appoint the Project Executive to the Project Management Team, they could in certain cases appoint the Project Manager and remainder of the Project Management Team.

The work undertaken as part of the SU process varies depending upon the project

Appointing the Executive and Project Manager

The Executive is appointed by the commissioning organization to represent the interests if the business stakeholders, The Executive has the decision-making authority over the project and the appointment is a pre-requisite ensuring the project is justified

The Executive appoints the Project Manager, with support and input from the Corp, Programme or Customer organization if required. The Project Manager manages the day-2-day operations of the project on the Executives behalf, the first task the Project Manager has it create the Daily Log

The Daily Log is created as a record of information about the project until more formal record keeping in in place

Capturing Lessons Learned

Previous Prince2 2017 projects are a source of information that can support future projects, these are contained within previous projects lessons logs, or end project reports. In certain cases, these may not be available and such information can be gathered by using workshops, meetings with members of the organization both internal or external. These lessons can detail both the strengths and weaknesses of previous processes, tools and techniques and are recorded within the lessons log

Design and appoint the Project Management Team

The Project Management Team is key to the overall success of the project and time should be taken to when assembling the Project Management Team. The principle of Defined Roles & Responsibilities provides a clear definition of each members role and how those roles interact as well as providing a clear set of boundaries showing clear definition between the respective roles, as projects often have the multiple roles covering similar tasks.

It is important to consider some of the following when designing the Project Management Team

- Role descriptions should be clearly documented and include the accountability structure within the project
- Consideration whether any members of the Project Board wish to delegate the Project Assurance role and create descriptions for the those delegated roles
- Understand the Team Manager role, the number of possible Team Managers or the Project Managers role as a possible Team Manager
- Project Support and the consideration as to whether this will be delegated by the Project Manager and what level of delegation
- The identification, selection and confirmation of the Project Management Team Members with the approval from the respective line managers and if required approval from Corp, Programme or Customer

Preparation of the Outline Business Case

The Outline Business Case is derived from the Project Mandate, but this may well be a general document given level of detail understood about the overall project. The specifics to support the Detailed Business Case will be completed within the Initiating a Project Process (IP)

The responsibility for the creation of the Outline Business Case lies with the Executive however it is often supported by the Project Manager and Subject Matter Experts, as a minimum it should include:

- The goals and rationale for the project as defined within the Project Mandate
- The sources of project funding
- Background information and lessons
- The Project Product Description, written by the Project Manager supported and in consultation with the Senior User and Executive

The Outline Business Case is reviewed by Project Assurance and could be reviewed at Organization level as part of the creation and approval process

Selection of the Project Approach and assemble the Project Brief

The Project Approach requires some decisions to be undertaken regarding the overall project and how it will be approached\delivered.

The way in which the work is to be conducted will depend on any customer or supplier standards, practices and guidelines; for example, any specific delivery approaches that may apply.

These should be captured in the project brief as part of the project approach, as they will influence the project approaches to be created in the initiating a project process. It also ensures that the project approach is clearly understood between customer and supplier and does not jeopardize the project in any way.

An agreed project brief ensures that the project has a commonly understood and well-defined start point, all stakeholders involved in the project at this point should be included in the creation and approval of the Project Brief and Project Approach.

Assembly of the Project Brief is a crucial key step in the Start-up of the project, the Project Brief defines the project, sets out the project approach and should include the chosen solution for the delivery of the project and should include:

- The project definition
- The current status of the project
- The projects goals and outcomes
- The project scope
- Any identified project constraints
- Project level tolerances
- Identified project users and stakeholders
- Outline Business Case
- Project Product Description
- Project Approach
- Project Management Team roles
- Project Management Team structure

Initiation Stage planning

The Starting Up a Project Process (SU) is used to plan the Initiation Stage, unlike the SU stage the Initiation Stage is often complex and requires time and resources. This work needs to be planned and focused.

The control and reporting for the stage should be paid particular focus. These should be clearly defined, and any risks associated identified

The final step of the Starting up a Project Process is to trigger the Directing a Project Process (DP) and request the approval to initiate the project, this approval is from the Project Board

Directing a Project Process (DP)

The purpose of the Directing a Project Process (abbreviated to DP) is to enable the project board to be accountable for the project's success by making key decisions and exercising overall control while delegating day-to-day management of the project to the project manager.

The Principle of Manage by Exception, the Project Board is only called upon to make decisions when the project falls outside of its pre-defined tolerances, or at key points within the projects lifecycle

The goals or objectives of the DP process is to ensure that there is authority to initiate the project, there is authority to deliver the project's products, management direction and control are provided throughout the project's life, the project remains viable, corporate, programme management or the customer has an interface to the project, there is authority to close the project and that plans for realizing the post-project benefits are managed and reviewed.

Activities within the Directing a Project Process

The DP Process is focused upon the Project Board and their responsibility for maintaining the projects Continued Business Justification Principle throughout the lifecycle of the project. The Project Board also provides formal and informal direction to the Project Manager, this is known as Ad-Hoc direction within a Prince2 2017 project

Authorizing Initiation

Projects by their nature require resources, this is time, money and physical resources to initiate, so the activities for initiation should be planned, monitored and controlled. The project board activity to authorize initiation ensures that such investment is worthwhile

When a request to initiate a project is received from Starting up a Project, the project board must decide whether to allow the project to proceed to the initiation stage

The request to initiate the project is sent to the Project Board at the end of the SU Process, the Project Board should review the Project Brief, which will include the Project Management Team Structure, the Project Product Description, the Outline Business Case and the Initiation Stage Plan.

If appropriate, the Project Board will approve the request to initiate and will then inform all stakeholders that the project has been initiated, and give the Project Manager permission to proceed to the Initiation Stage

Authorize the Project

This activity will be triggered by a request from the project manager for authorization to deliver the project and may be undertaken in parallel with authorizing a stage or exception plan

The objective of authorizing the project is to decide whether to proceed with the rest of the project. The Project Board will review the Project Initiation Documentation (PID) and use this information to determine if the project is achievable.

The Project Board will make the decision to approve the project, along with reviewing the PID the Project Board will also review the Benefits Management Approach, if the decision to authorise is approved confirmation will be given to Corporate, Program or Customer. The Project Manager will be given permission to proceed to next stage.

In the vent the project is no longer seen as justifiable, the Project Board will inform the Project Manager will be instructed to close the project

This is the first point in the projects lifecycle that the project can be prematurely closed

Authorizing a Stage or Exception Plan

It is important that a management stage starts only when the project board says it should.

The project board authorizes a management stage by reviewing the performance of the current stage and approving the stage plan for the next stage. Approval of stage plans occurs at the end of every management stage except the last one, where it is replaced by the Closing a Project Process (CP)

The Stage Plan should contain sufficient detail to allow the Project Manager to manage the stage, this is often now known until the close to when the stage is due to commence, hence the term the Next Stage Plan is not documented or commenced until near the end of the current stage

The Project Board must authorize the next management stage by approving the stage plan as part of the Managing a Stage Boundary Process (SB)

If an exception occurs, the Project Board is responsible for approving is responsible for approving the Exception Plan that is created by the Project Manager, which when approved will replace the current stage plan allowing the stage to be completed.

The Project Board may also decide to appoint Project Assurance to undertake some of the reviewing and assessment of the relevant documentation and where required liaise with Corporate, Programme or Customer

Ad-Hoc Direction
Within a Prince2 2017 project, it is expected that the Project Manager will seek informal guidance and consult frequently with the Project Board or the individual members when clarifications are needed.

During certain points in the projects lifecycle, it is envisaged that the liaison with the Project Board may increase, during the initiation stage or when a stage boundary is approaching for example, the Project Manager may need additional support or guidance from the members of the Project Board

It is also possible that corporate, programme management or the customer revises the project mandate in response to events external to the project or instructs the project board to close the project. The project board has two primary options should corporate, programme management or the customer decide to change the project mandate, they may treat it as a Change Request or to prematurely close the project

Authorizing Project Closure
A key factor within a Prince2 2017 project is that they have a defined start and end, it is important that projects do not continue on and on where they could become business as usual

Authorizing closure of the project is the last activity undertaken by the project board, prior to its own disbandment, and may require endorsement from corporate, programme management or the customer.

The project board may appoint Project Assurance to undertake some of the reviewing and assessing actions (e.g. inspecting the end project report to confirm it is accuracy).

The Project Board will
- Review and approve the End Project Report and assess the overall project performance. This will include and follow-on-recommendations and hand overs requirements to responsible parties
- Review and hand over the Lessons Report to Corporate, Programme or Customer
- Review the Benefits Management Approach and ensure that the updated benefits reviews are in place and cover the performance of the projects products in operational use to enable them to be assessed and any adverse effects are identified
- Confirm the updated Business Case by comparing the forecasted versus actual costs, risks, benefits against the Outline Business Case
- Review and issue the Project Closure Notification to the relevant stakeholders, this should include the date of closure and the project costs

Initiating a Project Process (IP)
The purpose of the initiating a project process abbreviated to IP, is to establish solid foundations for the project, enabling the organization to understand the work that needs to be done to deliver the project's products before committing any significant resources (time, manpower, specialist resources etc.)

This enables the Project Board to make an informed decision as to the projects viability

The goals of the IP Process are to define and document the reasons, benefits, costs, scope, resources needed, quality and any major risks that could affect or impact the projects delivery and achievement of benefits

The IP Stage is focused primarily upon the Project Manager, this stage will focus upon the Project Initiation Documentation (PID) and the Benefits Management Approach. These documents set the baselines for the project variables and the project controls

Activities of Initiating a Project Process

The activities within the initiating a project process are all project manager oriented and are to:

- Agree the tailoring requirements
- Prepare the Risk Management Approach
- Prepare the Change Control Approach
- Prepare the Quality Management Approach
- Prepare the Communication Management Approach
- Set up the project controls
- Create the project plan
- Refine the Business Case and create the Benefits Management Approach
- Assemble the Project Initiation Documentation
- Create the Next Stage Plan

The Project Manager will develop these documents to enable the project control, management processes which will then be approved by the Project Board as part of the Directing a Project Process (DP)

Tailoring

The project may need tailoring to suit the projects complexity or organization's needs. Any deviations from the organization's standard project management approach must be documented and agreed. These will be documented as part of the PID and form part of the Project Controls

Preparation of the Risk Management Approach

The preparation of the Risk Management Approach sets the goals of applying the risk management within the context of the actual project, the procedures that will be followed or adopted from the Corporate, Programme or Customer processes or procedures, the risk tolerances, the timings of any risk management activities, the tools and techniques that will be used.

It takes inputs from the Project Brief, the lessons from previous projects and the Corporate, Programme or Customer policies and procedures

Preparation of the Change Control Approach

Change control is essential for the project to maintain control over its management and specialist products, without this control the project is likely to experience scope creep and possibly overspend or delays

The level of control required will vary from project to project. The maximum level of control possible is determined by breaking down the project's products until the level is reached at which a component can be independently installed, replaced or modified. However, the level of control exercised will be influenced by the importance of the project and the complexity of the relationship between its products.

The change control approach will define the format and composition of the records that need to be maintained, it is a tool used for managing the products produced over the life of the project. It includes the change control procedure, procedures for the management of issues and changes, change control tools, technique, record keeping, reporting processes, reporting timings, roles and responsibilities

Prepare the Quality Management Strategy

The most critical success factor of any project is that it delivers what is expected of the user, and that is fit for purpose.

This will only be achieved if these expectations are agreed at the earliest point, this should ideally be in the beginning of the project but could be in later stages when more information is understood about the projects products.

The purpose of the Quality Management Approach is to ensure that any agreements are captured, it should also include any tailoring requirements, the approach to quality within the project, the roles and responsibilities, any tools or techniques that will be used and the Quality Management System details

Prepare the Communication Management Approach

The Communication Management Approach addresses communication both internal and external to the project. It contains details of how the Project Manager will communicate with stakeholders and receive information in relation to the project. If the project is part of a programme, this information should be received from the Programme Management Office and tailored to suit the project's needs, this tailoring is contained within the Project Controls

Prepare the Project Controls

The Project Controls allow the Project Board to practice the Principle of Manage by Exception and effectively minimize its involvement on a day-2-day basis during the projects lifecycle. This allows the Project Manager to manage the project on a daily basis

The Project Board makes the decisions at key points within the project, normally these are at Stage Boundaries or in exceptions, with this in mind it is key that stages are agreed and documented, the levels of delegation or decision making, roles and responsibilities within the project, the frequency of communication between the Project Board and project management levels, mechanisms to capture and monitor issues, changes, monitor tolerances and escalate exceptions

Create the Project Plan

The Project Plan within a Prince2 2017 project is more than a Gannt Chart, the project plan documents the requirements, the timeline, resources requirements.

Although the Project Manager is responsible for creating the Project Plan, planning should not be completed in isolation, rather it should be done with the support of other within the project and also external to it if required.

The Project Brief and Project Product Descriptions should be reviewed as the starting point for the Project Plan along with any Corp, Programme or Customer guidelines or templates that relate to the Project Plan

Roles and Responsibilities should be assigned, risks identified and documented, the project controls should be spelled out in details to remove any possible ambiguity

Refining the Business Case

The Outline Business Case created as part of the SU Process is revisited and expanded, the responsibility for the Business Case lies with the Executive, however the expansion and work to complete this is often completed by the Project Manager with support again from subject matter experts

The outline business case needs to be updated to reflect the estimated time and costs, as determined by the project plan, and the risks identified as part of the detailed planning process contained within the updated risk register.

The detailed business case will be used by the project board to authorize the project and provides the basis of the ongoing check that the project remains viable. For more details on business justification

The final Business Case is supported by the Benefits Management Approach, that contains details on how the benefits will be recorded, the baselines aligned to the benefits that will be measured, ongoing benefit measurements, the timings for each benefit review and the roles and responsibilities aligned to the benefit reviews

The Business Case is the Project Boards primary information source when it makes the decision to authorise the project and also serves as the primary basis for continued evaluation when reviewing the projects Continued Business Justification

Assemble the Project Initiation Documentation (PID)

The PID is the focal point for the project and contains the What, Why, who, how, where, when and most importantly how much and is important to remember, the PID is not a single document but the consolidation of the following documents:

1. Project Definition
2. Project Approach
3. Project Management Team Structure
4. Role Descriptions
5. Quality Management Approach
6. Chance Control Approach
7. Risk Management Approach
8. Communication Management Approach
9. Project Plan
10. Project Controls
11. Detailed Business Case
12. Project Tailoring

The Benefits Management Approach is separate from the PID, whilst it is crucial to the creation of the Business Case and directly supports it. The Benefits Management Approach is the only document that continues post project.

Plan the Next Stage

Upon completion of the assembly of the PID with the approved documents. The Project Manager will then create the Stage Plan for the next management stage.

This will be the basis for the day-2-day management of the project used by the Project Manager

The creation of this document is the trigger for the Managing a Stage Boundary Process whereby the Project Board will make the decision to Authorize the Project as part of the Directing a Project Process

Managing a Stage Boundary Process

The purpose of the Managing a Stage Boundary Process abbreviated to SB is used to break the project into management stages, these stages provide the basis for the projects control and enable the Project Board to review the projects progress and its Continued Business Justification

The managing a stage boundary process enables the project manager to provide the project board with sufficient information to be able to:

- Review the success of the current management stage
- Approve the next stage plan
- Review the updated project plan
- Confirm continued business justification and acceptability of the risks.

This process should be executed at or near the end of the current management stage allowing the Project Board to review the success of the current stage and to approve the commencement of the next stage

The Managing a Stage Boundary Process is focused upon the Project Manager who provides the Project Board with the information needed to review the project and approve the projects progress to the next stage. It is crucial the Project Manager provides the Project Board sufficient time to review the documentation required to make this assessment and approval

The Stage Boundary process is mandatory at the end of each management stage, the only variation is the final stage where the Stage Boundary is replaced with the Closing a Project Process (CP)

If the project goes out of tolerance at any point, the Project Manager will prepare an Exception Report for the Project Board. If the exception is at stage level, the Project Board may request an Exception Plan from the Project Manager to allow the stage to be completed. The Exception Plan is presented to the Project Board in the same manner as the Stage Plan

A stage level exception is different than a project level exception, in the event the exception is at project level, the Project Board must escalate the Exception Plan to Corp, Programme or Customer for approval before the project can proceed

Activities of Managing a Stage Boundary

Planning the next stage
The Stage Plan for the next Management Stage is created at or near the end of the current management stage, planning is not undertaken alone and is undertaken in consultation with the Project Boar, Project Assurance and subject matter experts

The Project Manager will review the contents of the PID and if required update the documents with the most up to date and accurate information, approval from the Project Board may be necessary for these changes

The Project Manage will create the plan for the next Management Stage

Update the Project Plan
As part of each stage boundary, the Project manager will review the Project Plan to enable the Project Board to have the information needed to assess and measure the projects progress.

The review should include:
- Check that the current stage plan is up to date with actual progress and update it if necessary.
    - Revise the project plan to reflect:
        - Actuals from the current stage plan forecasts from the next stage plan, or the impact of the exception plan
        - Any changes to the project product description
        - The implications of any issues or risks
        - Any new or changed PRINCE2 process-tailoring requirements for the project
        - Any changed or extra products sanctioned by the project board
        - Any changes within the PID (e.g. revised project approaches, project controls, project management team structure or role descriptions).
- Update the issue register and risk register if any new issues or risks have been identified (or if existing ones need to be modified).

Update the Business Case
The Prince2 2017 principle of Continued Business Justification, the Project Manager will review and where necessary update the Business Case to reflect the most accurate and up to date information and reflects any changes during the stage or the projects lifecycle

The Executive has the ultimate responsibility for the Business Case as the financial stakeholder and representative of the Business, and will be consulted as part of the review and also be an approver of any changes

The revisions are submitted for approval from the Project Board, as they include changes to the projects risk profile, timelines, cost profile and in extreme circumstances, the benefits profile

Report Management Stage End

The Project Manager will prepare the End Stage Report to enable the Project Board to evaluate the projects progress and the success of the current stage. Reporting the stage end should only occur at the end of the stage and not close to the end!

Reporting stage end includes a review of the Business Case and the PID, a verification of the Benefits Management Approach and that all products from the current stage are completed or are included where necessary in the plan for the next stage

This information is contained within the End Stage Report, that is then submitted to the Project Board in conjunction with the next Stage Plan and a request for approval to close the current stage and proceed to the next stage

Produce an Exception Plan (If necessary)

If the project or stage is forecasted to exceed an agreed tolerance, the Project Manager must compile an Exception Report for the Project Board to review, the Project Board will then review and request an Exception Plan from the Project Manager

If approved, the Exception Plan replaces the current Stage Plan to allow the stage to be completed. The replacement of any Stage Plan must be approved by the Project Board, in the event the Project Plan is replaced, this may be subject to a review and approval from Corp, Programme or Customer dependent upon the levels of authority that has been granted to the Project Board

The creation of an Exception Plan requires consultation with the Project Board, Team Managers and Project Assurance or any other stakeholders as required and should include:
- Review and update the Issue Register ensuring the request for the plan is recorded
- Review the contents of the PID and update as necessary, where required request approvals from the Project Board
- Produce the Exception Plan and update all planning documents upon approval from the Project Board

Controlling a Stage Process

The purpose of the Controlling a Stage Process abbreviated to CS, is to assign work to be done, monitor such work, deal with issues, report progress to the project board, and take corrective actions to ensure that the management stage remains within tolerance.

The main goal of the CS Process is to reduce or avoid any possible scope creep, ensuring the effort of the Project Management Team is focused upon the products being delivered within the approved stage.

CS effectively focuses upon the delivery of the products in compliance or conformity with the defined tolerances set by the Project Board for Time, Cost Quality. The Project Manager will also review constantly review the Business Case and manage issues and risks during the stage

The Project Manager will create the Work Packages as part of the CS Process, the Work Package defines the work needed to create the product and the quality requirements that need to be met for its approval and acceptance. Work Packages allow for the communication of the tolerances for each stage or product to the Team Manager.

In the event the Project Manager is fulfilling the role of Team Manager, Work Packages are still used. In this scenario the references to the Team Manager within the Work Package will reference the individual team members and not the Project Manager

The first CS Process is the stage after approval to deliver the project is received from the Project Board, however Prince2 2017 also recommends or states that the CS Process is open and available to use during the Initiating a Project Process in projects where the initiation is expected to be long and complicated

Activities of Controlling a Stage

The CS process can be divided into three categories and these are all undertaken from the perspective of the Project Manager

- Work Packages
  - Authorise Work Package
  - Review Work Package status
  - Receive completed Work Package
- Monitoring and Reporting
  - Review stage status
  - Reporting project highlights
- Issues and Risks
  - Capture, examine issues and risks
  - Escalate issues and risks
  - Take corrective actions

Work Packages

This is the method that enables the Project Manager to control the work being undertaken on behalf of the project, if people assigned were to start work as and when they wished the project would rapidly become chaotic!

Each product should have a work package and only a single work package, if the product requires more than one, it should be broken into separate work packages each with its own Product Description. No work can be undertaken until the Project Manager grants the permission to start and this permission is in the form of a Work Package

The Work Package process consists of 3 steps, Authorize, Review and Receive:

Authorize Work Package: The Project Manager defines the Work Package in detail and this information is derived from the Project Product Description, the Product Description and any secondary information to support the Work Package from subject matter experts assigned to the project. The Project Manager will review the Work Package with the Team Manager, who will then accept it its current state or after changes requested as part of the review process. Once accepted by the Team Manager, the Project Manager will authorize the Team Manage to commence working upon the Work Package and create the respective product

Review Work Package Status: The Project Manager will review the status of the Work Package whilst the Team Manager is managing the delivery of the product ensuring the time and effort are in line with the estimates. The progress is reported upon using the Checkpoint Report which should contain information upon the progress, quality information, risks and issues

Receive Completed Work Package: Once the Work Package has been completed, the Project Manager will formally accept this as a completed work package. This will follow acceptance by the representative of the Senior User defined within the Work Package, usually in the form of a Quality Review

Monitoring and Reporting

The Project Managers main responsibility is to maintain control of the project ensuring an accurate record of the work is maintained ensuring that the resources are not over assigned or adversely underutilized! The monitoring and reporting provides a clear overview of the progress within the project and the current stage and monitors risk, issues and any potential areas of concern in relation to tolerances

Monitoring and reporting predominantly includes 2 areas:

Reviewing Stage Status:
Reviewing the Stage Plan provides the Project Manager with a view of how this stage is progressing, Reviewing the stage can be either part of the daily tasks undertaken by the Project Manager or by request of the Project Board.

If the project is not monitored on a regular basis, there is an obvious risk that it will proceed in an uncontrolled fashion, reviewing the stage provides the ability to make both timely and informed decision and maintain control

Reviewing is undertaken by:
- Reviewing checkpoint reports for the current period
- Review the current stage plan forecast against actuals
- Request a product status account from project support to identify any variation between planned progress, reported progress and actual progress
- Check for any quality issues shown in the quality register
- Check the risk register for any new or revised risks and assess their impact on the business case, stage   plan or project plan
- Check the issue register to see whether anything has happened within the project or externally that will impact on the business case, stage plan or project plan
- Check the status of any corrective actions
- Assess the utilization of resources in the period under review and their availability for the remainder of   the management stage (or project). Check for any variation in the expected future resource availability
- Check the benefits management approach to see whether any benefits management actions are due and execute them as necessary.

Based upon this the Project Manager can undertake a number of actions,
- Authorize a work package
- Report highlights in accordance with the communication management approach
- Capture and examine issues and risks
- Escalate issues and risks if tolerances are threatened
- Take corrective action
- Seek project board advice (and if necessary provide the project board with the issue report)
- Log any lessons that have been identified
- Continue as planned.

Reporting Highlights:
The Project Manager will supply the Project Board with information relating to the project relating to progress, issues, risks and possibly finances relating to the current stage and the overall project.

The overall reporting is controlled and documented within the Communication Management Approach during the IP Process

To provide this information the Project Manager will:
- Assemble the information from the checkpoint reports, risk register, issue register, quality register, lessons log, product status account and any significant revisions to the stage plan for the current reporting period (the information is gained from the review of the management stage status)
- Assemble a list of corrective actions (as noted in the daily log and/or recorded in the issue register) undertaken during the reporting period. This will, for example, assure the project board that the project manager is acting within the agreed tolerances (the information is gained from taking corrective action)
- Review the highlight report for the previous reporting period. Produce the highlight report for the current reporting period.
- Distribute the highlight report to the project board and any other recipients identified in the communication management approach.

Capturing and examining issues and risks

The very nature of Projects means that very few of them will be completed without issues or risks occurring during their lifecycle. These issues and risks will arrive in an ad-hoc manner from potential any stakeholder involved within the project, or even external to the project.

Before any decision is made as to how to deal with the issue or risk, it should be registered and assessed to understand its impact upon the projects objectives.

The steps that should be used when managing issues or risks are: Capture, Examine, Escalate and Take corrective action

- *Capture and examine issues and risks*: Issues and Risks within the project will be received in a nice orderly fashion and often they will come randomly and because of the Project Manager needs a method to capture and record the issues and risks.

  Before any decision can be taken as to how to manage the issue or risk, it must be registered and assessed to understand its impact, the Project Manager should:

  For issues that need to be managed formally
  - Check the requirements of the issue management and change control procedure in the change control approach
  - Manage the issue in accordance with the Change Control Approach
  - Report the status of the issue in accordance with the Change Control Approach and check the Communication Management Approach to see whether there are any external parties that need to be informed of the issue.

  For risks
  - Check the requirements of the risk management procedure within the Risk Management Approach
  - Manage the risk in accordance with the process documented within the Risk Management Approach
  - Report the status of the risk in accordance with the Risk Management Approach and check the Communication Management Approach to see whether there are any external parties that need to be informed of the risk.

If necessary to take corrective actions, seek advice from the Project Board or escalate the Project Manager should review the management stage and its current status to understand the full picture

- *Escalate issues and risks*: A management stage should not exceed the tolerances agreed with the project board. The project manager can only take corrective action or maintain the status quo as long as the management stage (or project) is forecast to be completed within the tolerances set by the project board.

  This activity applies where any corrective action within the project manager's control would not save the management stage (or project) from going beyond the tolerances agreed. This applies to all types of issue and risk (or aggregations of them) that cannot be resolved within the tolerances set by the project board.

  This issue or risk is escalated in the form of an exception report to the Project Board, the exception report describes the situation, the options available and if possible the recommended course of action. The Project Board will them make a decision as to which course of action should be taken, this could include changes the tolerances or requesting an Exception Plan or prematurely closing the project

- *Taking corrective action*: if the issue or risk will not affect the stage or project and they will remain within the agreed tolerances, the Project Manager should manage the issues and risks through the corrective action at the management level. The corrective action should solve the problem within the need to exceed the agreed tolerances.

The Project Manager should seek the input and guidance from the Project Board as part of the Ad-Hoc direction when considering the options to resolve the issue or risk. The Project Manager should also use the information contained within the Issue or Risk Register, Configuration Item Records and the Daily Log to gather as much information relating to the selection of the corrective action

The corrective actions are documented in the form of a revised or new Work Package and the Project Manager should update the Configuration Item Records, the Issue Report and the Issue Register to reflect the updated status and any revisions or changes

It may also be necessary to update the Project Product Description or Product Descriptions

Managing Product Delivery

The purpose of the Managing Product Delivery abbreviated to MP, is to control the link between the Project Manager and the Team Manager(s), whereas the CS Process is focused upon the Project Manager, the MP Process is focused upon the Team Manager and the job of actually creating the specialist products required by the project. The MP Process also provides a focal point for the direction or management of 3rd party or external suppliers

The objectives of the MP Process are to ensure that:
- Team managers, team members and suppliers are clear as to what
  is to be produced and

  what is the expected effort, cost or timescales
- The planned products are delivered to expectations and within
  tolerance
- Accurate progress information is provided to the project manager
  at an agreed frequency to ensure that expectations are managed

Activities of the Managing Product Delivery Process

The activities of the MP process are orientated towards the Team Manager are:
- Accept a Work Package
- Execute a Work Package
- Deliver a Work Package

The Team Manager is central point of contact and management in relation to the Work Packages and the creation of the project products. The Team Manager receives the Work Package from the Project Manager and creates the Team Plan. The Team Manager then tracks all quality activities and obtains approval for the completed products before delivering them to the Project Manager

Accepting a Work Package

The fundamental principle is that a Work Package should be agreed between the Project Manager and the Team Manager before it is allocated. The Work Package should contain the details of the Work Package or Packages, the deliverable information, any known limitations or constraints, procedures to be followed.

The Team Manager will review the Work Package and discuss any specifics or changes\clarifications with the Project Manager to adjust or modify any tolerances and agree reporting requirements and approval\acceptance procedures

The Team Manager will then produce the Team Plan which will demonstrate how the products will be produced within the agreed parameters\constraints and if required seek clarifications from Project Assurance

The Project Manager will then formally agree the Team Plan and Authorise the Work Package. In the scenario where the Team Plan is from an external or 3rd party supplier, it may not be necessary to approve the team plan

Execute a Work Package:
The Team Manager will oversee the work of producing the product in alignment with the agreed Work Package and monitor the results. During the process of producing the products the team Manager will report upon the progress to the Team Manager using the Checkpoint Report according to the agreed frequency and contents

In the event any tolerances are exceeded, The Team Manager must report the issue to the Project Manager and should also update the Quality Register relating to the Work Package, obtain approval for the completed work package using the Quality Review Technique and update the Team Plan to reflect that it has been completed and accepted

Deliver a Work Package:
Upon completion of the Work Package and acceptance by the representatives of the Senior User, The Team Manager will inform the Project Manager. The Team Manager will update the Quality Register and Team Plan ensuring that all quality processes and procedures have been followed

Closing a Project Process
The Closing a Project Process abbreviated to CP, is the final stage within a Prince2 2017 project. The purpose of the CP Process is to provide a fixed point at which acceptance of the project's product is confirmed, and to recognize that objectives set out in the original PID have been achieved (or approved changes to the objectives have been achieved), or that the project has nothing more to contribute. The CP Process may also be used if the project is prematurely closed or stopped

The objectives of the CP Process are to confirm user acceptance of all products relating to the project, and to review the finished products conformance in comparison to the projects baselines established within the PID. A key clarification is that the organisation can support the product after the projects organization is dissolved and providing clarification of any outstanding issues or risks that require follow-on-actions

The CP process is primarily focused upon the Project Manager who will oversee the closure of the project, receipt of all approvals and acceptances relating to the project products

The Project Manager will recommend to the Project Board that the project is closed, the Project Board and ultimately the Executive will authorise the closure of the project.

The Executive will notify the Project Manager that the project is closed and notify the Corp, Programme or Customer that the project has been closed.

The CP Process should be built into the stage plan for the final management stage

Activities of the Closing a Project Process
The activities of the CP process are orientated to the Project Manager and are:

- Prepare planned closure
- Prepare premature closure
- Hand over products
- Evaluate the project
- Recommend project closure

Prepare Planned Closure:
Before closure of the project can be recommended, the project manager must ensure that the expected results have all been achieved and delivered. This is done by:
- Updating the project plan with actuals from the final management stage.
- Request a product status account from project support. From the product status account, ensure that the

- project's products: have been approved by the authorities identified in their product descriptions
- meet all the quality criteria or are covered by approved concessions.
- Confirm that the project has delivered what is defined in the project product description, and that the acceptance criteria have been met.
- Seek approval to give notice to corporate, programme management or the customer that resources can be (or are about to be) released.

Prepare Premature Closure:
In some situations, the project board may instruct the Project Manager to close the project prematurely.

In such circumstances, the project manager must ensure that work in progress is not simply abandoned, but that the project salvages anything of value created to date and checks that any gaps left by the cancellation of the project are raised to corporate, programme management or the customer.

Any gaps created by closing the project prematurely must be documented and provided to Corp, Programme or Customer

The Project Manager will:
- Update the issue register (and, if necessary, the issue report) to record the premature closure request.
- Update the project plan with actuals from the final management stage.
- Request a product status account from project support. From this, determine which of the project's products:
  - have been approved by the authorities identified in their product descriptions are currently in development (and which of those need to be completed)
  - are covered by approved concessions
  - have yet to be started
  - need to be made safe may be useful to other projects.
- Agree the means for recovering products that have been completed or are in progress (if appropriate). This will need project board consultation and may include additional work to create, make safe or complete products that might be useful to other projects (e.g. making an unfinished building safe and weatherproof). In some cases, the additional work may require an exception plan.
- Seek approval to give notice to corporate, programme management or the customer that resources can be (or are about to be) released early.

Hand over Products:
The specialist products created by the project must be handed over to the operational and maintenance environment prior to the projects closure, this can happen as a single release or as a phased release during the development cycle. If required, the Benefits Management Approach should be updated to reflect the usage of the products and ensure any lessons learned are documented. Any service or maintenance agreements should be implemented within the final phase of the project, this is critical to ensuring the projects products are handed over and maintained ensuring that the benefits are achieved

Evaluate the Project:
The evaluation of the project will assess how successful or unsuccessful the project is with the intention of gathering lessons learned to support future projects and support the improvement of Corp. Programme or Customer processes in relation to the project delivery process

The original PID provides a baseline for the Project Manager to evaluate the project comparing the final product and objectivise against the original baselines. The Project Manager will then prepare the End Project Report with support from the Project Management Team, this will include a Lessons Learned Report and when completed, is submitted to the Project Board with a recommendation to close the project and disband the project organization

Recommend Project Closure:

Upon confirming that the project has delivered all of the specialist products and that they have been accepted into both the operational and maintenance environments, the Project Manager determines that the project is ready to be closed and makes the recommendation in writing to the Project Board and primarily the Executive.

The Project Manager will:
- Use the communication management approach to identify any organization or interested party who needs to know that the project is closing.
- Consider also communication activities for public relations and marketing opportunities at this point.
- Close the project's issue register, risk register, quality register, daily log and lessons log.
- Make sure that all project information is secured and archived (in accordance with the change control approach) in order to permit any future audit of the project management team's decisions, actions and performance.
- Prepare and send a draft project closure notification for review by the project board, stating that the project has closed.

Prince2 2017 – Tailoring

The seventh principle within Prince2 2017 is Tailoring and it states that Prince2 2017 should be tailored to suit the project and the project environment

The primary goal is to apply a level of project management that does not overburden the Project Management Team but provides an appropriate level of governance and control, at an acceptable level of risk

Tailoring can be done in two ways:
- If an organization does not have its own project management method, tailoring will be done directly from the PRINCE2 manual.
- If an organization has its own PRINCE2-based project management method, this will be tailored to suit the project.

Within Prince2 2017, there is now a focus upon the ability to tailor Prince2 2017, and it is primarily concerned with the appropriate use of Prince2 2017 on any given project.

The following can aspects can be tailored:
- Processes may be combined or adapted (e.g. by adding or combining activities).
- Themes can be applied using techniques that are appropriate to the project.
- Roles may be combined or split, provided that accountability is maintained and there are no conflicts of interest.
- Management products may be combined or split into any number of documents or data sources. They will often take the form of formal documents, but can equally be slide decks, wall charts or data held on IT systems if more appropriate to the project and its environment.
- Terminology may be changed to suit other standards or policies, provided it is applied consistently.

Within the revised manual, there is a focus on the minimum requirements to be a Prince2 2017 project, these will be highlighted in the next chapters

Tailoring Themes

Tailoring the Business Case Theme

The purpose of the business case theme is to establish the mechanisms to judge whether the project is (and remains) desirable, viable and achievable as a means to support decision-making in its (continued) investment.

To be following PRINCE2, a project must, as a minimum:
- Create and maintain a business justification for the project; usually a business case (supporting the Continued Business Justification Principle)
- Review and update the business justification in response to decisions and events that might impact desirability, viability or achievability of the project (supporting the Continued Business Justification Principle)
- Define the management actions that will be put in place to ensure that the project's outcomes are achieved and confirm that the project's benefits are realized (PRINCE2's continued business justification principle)
- Define and document the roles and responsibilities for the business case and benefits management (PRINCE2's defined roles and responsibilities principle).

PRINCE2 requires that two products are produced and maintained for the business case theme:
- The Business Case: Provides the costs, benefits, expected dis-benefits, risks and timescales against which viability is justified and continuing viability is tested. It is acceptable to use an alternative document such as a corporate business plan to replace the business case for part of the project lifecycle.

- **The Benefits Management Approach:** Defines the management actions that will be put in place to ensure that the project's outcomes are achieved and confirm that the project's benefits are realized.

In PRINCE2 the business case is developed at the beginning of the project. Throughout the life of the project the business case is reviewed and updated as it develops and evolves. It is formally verified by the project board at each key decision point, such as at stage boundaries, and confirmed throughout the period that benefits accrue.

Appendix A of the P2 Manual provides product descriptions and suggested content for these products.

Tailoring the Organisation Theme
The purpose of the Organization Theme is to define and establish the projects structure of accountability and responsibility

To be following PRINCE2, a project must, as a minimum:
- Define its organization structure and roles. This must minimally ensure that all of the responsibilities in PRINCE2's role descriptions are fulfilled (Supporting Prince2 2017's Defined Roles and Responsibilities Principle)
- Document the rules for delegating change authority responsibilities, if required
- Define its approach to communicating and engaging with stakeholders.

PRINCE2 requires that two products are produced and maintained for the organization theme:
- **Project Initiation Documentation (PID):** In the context of the Organization Theme, this provides the single source of reference for how the project is to be managed. The PID sets out the Project Management Team structure and roles.
- **Communication Management Approach** This describes the means and frequency of communication to stakeholders both internal and external to the project.

Both these products should be created during the Initiating a Project Process.

Appendix A of the P2 Manual provides product descriptions and suggested content for these products.

Tailoring the Quality Theme
The purpose of the Quality Theme is to define and implement the means by which the project will verify that products are fit for purpose
To be following PRINCE2, a project must, as a minimum:
- Define its quality management approach. This approach must minimally cover:
  - The project's approach to quality control the project's approach to project assurance
  - How the management of quality is communicated throughout the project lifecycle
  - The roles and responsibilities for quality management (Supporting Prince2 2017's Defined Roles and Responsibilities Principle)
- Specify explicit quality criteria for products in their product descriptions (Supporting Prince2 2017's Focus on Products Principle)
- Maintain records to provide evidence that the planned quality activities have been carried out, and summarize those activities that are planned or have taken place in some form of Quality Register
- Specify the customer's quality expectations and prioritized acceptance criteria for the project in the Project Product Description
- Use lessons to inform quality planning, the definition of quality expectations and quality criteria (PRINCE2's learn from experience principle).

PRINCE2 requires that two products are produced and maintained:
- **Quality Management Approach**: A quality management approach describes how quality will be managed on the project.

- o   This includes the specific processes, procedures, techniques, standards and responsibilities to be applied
- **Quality Register**: A quality register is used to summarize all the quality management activities that are planned or have taken place and provides information for the end stage reports and end project report

Appendix A of the P2 Manual provides product descriptions and suggested content for these products.

Tailoring the Plans Theme

The purpose of the Plans Theme is to facilitate and control by defining the means of delivering the products (the where, how and by whom and estimating the when and how much)

To be following PRINCE2, a project must, as a minimum:
- Ensure that plans enable the business case to be realized (Supporting Prince2 2017's Continued Business Justification Principle)
- Have at least two management stages: an initiation stage and at least one further management stage.
  - The more complex and risky a project, the more management stages that will be required (Supporting Prince2 2017'sPRINCE2's manage by stages principle)
- Produce a project plan for the project as a whole and a stage plan for each management stage (Supporting Prince2 2017's Manage by Stages Principle)
- Use product-based planning for the project plan, stage plans and exception plans. It may be optionally used for team plans.
- Produce specific plans for managing exceptions (Supporting Prince2 2017's Manage by Exception Principle)
- Define the roles and responsibilities for planning (Supporting Prince2 2017's Defined Roles & Responsibilities Principle)
- Use lessons to inform planning (Supporting Prince2 2017's Learn from Experience Principle).

PRINCE2 requires that four products are produced and maintained:

Project Product Description: A description of the overall project's output, including the customer's quality expectations, together with the acceptance criteria and acceptance methods for the project. As such it applies to a project plan only.

Product Description: A description of each product's purpose, composition, derivation and quality criteria.

Product Breakdown Structure: A hierarchy of all the products to be produced during a plan.

Plan: Provides a statement of how and when objectives are to be achieved, by showing the major products, activities and resources required for the scope of the plan. In PRINCE2, there are three levels of plan: project, stage and team. In addition, PRINCE2 has exception plans, which are created at the same level as the plan they are replacing.

Prince2 2017 recommends, but does not require, that an additional product is created and maintained:

Product flow diagram. This is a diagram showing the sequence of production and interdependencies of the products listed in a product breakdown structure.

Appendix A of the P2 Manual provides product descriptions and suggested content for these products.

Tailoring the Risk Theme

The purpose of the Risk Theme is to identify, assess and control uncertainty and, as a result improve the ability of the project to succeed

To be following PRINCE2, a project must, as a minimum:

Define its **risk management approach,** which must minimally cover:
- How risks are identified and assessed, how risk management responses are planned and implemented   and how the management of risk is communicated throughout the project lifecycle
- Assessing whether identified risks might have a material impact on the business justification of the project (Supporting Prince2 2017's Continued Business Justification Principle)

- The roles and responsibilities for risk management (Supporting Prince2 2017's Defined Roles & Responsibilities Principle)
- Maintain some form of risk register to record identified risks and decisions relating to their analysis, management and review
- Ensure that project risks are identified, assessed, managed and reviewed throughout the project lifecycle use lessons to inform risk identification and management (Supporting Prince2 2017's Learn from Experience Principle).

Prince2 2017 requires that two products are produced and maintained:
- **Risk Management Approach**: Describes how risk will be managed on the project. This includes the specific processes, procedures, techniques, standards and responsibilities to be applied.
- **Risk Register:** Provides a record of identified risks relating to the project, including their status and history. It is used to capture and maintain information on all the identified threats and opportunities relating to the project.

Both of these products should be created during the Initiating a Project Process.

The Risk Management Approach should be reviewed and possibly updated at the end of each management stage. The Risk Management Approach will define how and when the risk register is reviewed and updated.

Appendix A of the P2 Manual provides product descriptions and suggested content for these products.

Tailoring the Change Theme
The purpose of the Change Theme is to identify, assess and control any potential and approved changes to the project baselines

To be following PRINCE2, a project must, as a minimum:
- Define its **Change Control Approach.** This approach must minimally cover: how issues are identified and managed
  - assessing whether identified issues might have a material impact on the business justification of the project (Supporting Prince2 2017's Continued Business Justification Principle)
  - The roles and responsibilities for change control (Supporting Prince2 2017's Defined Roles and Responsibilities Principle), including a defined change authority
- Define how product baselines are created, maintained and controlled
- Maintain some form of **Issue Register** to record identified issues and decisions relating to their analysis,
- Management and review ensure that project issues are captured, examined, managed and reviewed throughout the project lifecycle use lessons to inform issue identification and management (Supporting Prince2 2017's Learn from Experience Principle)

PRINCE2 requires that the following products are produced and maintained:
Issue Register: Captures and maintains information on all the issues that are being formally managed.
Change Control Approach: Identifies how, and by whom, the project's products will be controlled and protected.

If the issue register does not contain sufficient detail (e.g. for the options appraisal, recommendation and decision), then a separate issue report, can be used but this is an optional management product.

The project's controls for issues and change will be defined and established during the initiating a project process, then reviewed and (if necessary) updated towards the end of each management stage by the managing a stage boundary process.

Appendix A of the P2 Manual provides product descriptions and suggested content for these products.

Tailoring the Progress Theme

The purpose of the progress theme is to establish mechanisms to monitor and compare actual achievements against those planned, provide a forecast for the project objectives and the project's continued viability, and control any unacceptable deviations.

To be following PRINCE2, a project must, as a minimum:

- Define its approach to controlling progress in the PID be managed by stages (Supporting Prince2 2017's Manage by Stages Principle)
- Set tolerances and be managed by exception against these tolerances (Supporting Prince2 2017's Manage by Exception Principle)
- Review the business justification when exceptions are raised (Supporting Prince2 2017's Continued Business Justification Principle)
- Learn lessons (Supporting Prince2 2017's Learn from Experience Principle)

PRINCE2 provides progress control through:

- Delegating authority from one level of management to the level below it
- Dividing the project into management stages and authorizing the project one management stage at a time (Supporting Prince2 2017's Manage by Stages Principle)
- Time-driven and event-driven progress reporting and reviews raising exceptions (Supporting Prince2 2017's Manage by Exception Principle)

The project's controls should be documented in the PID as part of the Initiating a Project Process.

Tailoring Process

Tailoring the Starting Up a Project Process

The purpose of the starting up a project process is to ensure that the prerequisites for initiating a project are in place by answering the question: Do we have a viable and worthwhile project? The decision to start the project must be explicit; the activities from starting up a project happen before this decision.

Nothing should be done until certain base information needed to make rational decisions about the commissioning of the project is defined, key roles and responsibilities are resourced and allocated, and a foundation for detailed planning is available.

The purpose of the starting up a project process is as much about preventing poorly conceived projects from ever being initiated as it is about approving the initiation of viable projects. As such, starting up a project is a lighter process compared to the more detailed and thorough initiating a project process. The aim is to do the minimum necessary in order to decide whether it is worthwhile to even initiate the project.

General Considerations

The activities in this process may be combined, split or run concurrently to suit the context, but care should be taken to ensure the integrity of the interface with the directing a project process when a request to initiate a project is submitted.

At this point in the project lifecycle, it may not always be clear what output the project is intended to create; if this is the case, it should at least be clear what business problem is to be solved or what outcome is required.

Tailoring Products within the Starting Up a Project Process

Lessons Log	Capturing of previous lessons is required as part of the PRINCE2 principle of learn from experience, although it may vary in respect of the formality used.

Project Brief, comprising:
    Outline Business Case
    Project Product Description
	The project brief may be a single document and it may reference corporate, portfolio, programme or customer documentation or reports, such as a feasibility report. It may range from being a simple statement describing the project to a fuller description.

	The team structure may only be partially complete at this point in time. Any management team structure is allowable as long as organization constraints are respected (see Chapter 7). The options and solutions may not yet be defined, in which case the project approach should describe how these will be determined. Role descriptions may be in any form. If formal role descriptions exist (e.g. as part of an organization's method) only a summary may be needed together with a reference to where the detail is. Alternatively, the role description may itself be amended to suit the needs of the project. The outline business case may range from being a simple statement of why the project is needed to a more detailed analysis and description. The project product description may include a statement of desired outcomes, relating to solving a business problem, if the solution products have not yet been identified.
Stage Plan (Initiating Stage)	The plan may include components in any format commensurate with the complexity of the project, with views such as a simple list of accountabilities, products, activities and dates or Gantt chart. The plan may be held totally or partially within a planning tool(s). The management product descriptions within a stage plan can themselves be tailored to suit the project.

Tailoring the roles within the Starting Up a Project Process

If a project manager has not been appointed at the start of this process, the required management products may be created by the executive or anyone appointed by them. Similarly, the executive does not need to create the outline business case personally but may have another person create this. The single point of accountability for each role's duty should be maintained.

Tailoring the Directing a Project Process

The purpose of the directing a project process is to enable the project board to be accountable for the project's success by making key decisions and exercising overall control while delegating day-to-day management of the project to the project manager

General Considerations

After approval to initiate the project has been confirmed, care should be taken to ensure the integrity of the interface to the initiating a project, managing a stage boundary and closing a project processes when the formal decision to start the next management stage or close the project is made

The degree of formality may differ in different circumstances provided decisions are explicit and traceable, ranging from verbal advice and decisions to those which are formally documented in email, meeting minutes or other traceable formats

Tailoring Roles within the Directing a Project Process

All the activities in this process are the accountability of the executive but the actual work may be done by others. It should, however, be noted that the project manager should not take any decisions or give approval or direction on matters which are the responsibility of the executive; the roles of executive and project manager must be kept separate

In some contexts, the decision at stage boundaries, particularly when funds are released for the next stage, may be taken by a role at a higher level than the executive, such as in a programme, portfolio or organization context.

For this reason, the 'authorize stage or exception plan' activity may be treated as a separate process in a tailored PRINCE2 process model.

Tailoring the Initiating Project Process

The purpose of the initiating a project process is to establish solid foundations for the project, enabling the organization to understand the work that needs to be done to deliver the project's products before committing to a significant spend.

General Considerations

The activities in this process may be combined, split or run concurrently to suit the project's circumstances.

The number of management products created in this process can look daunting and, together, may imply a level of detail that is not always needed. This process lays the foundation and it is here that tailoring for the project is primarily decided.

Tailoring is needed to suit a project's circumstances, but it may not always be obvious, at the start of initiation, what the relevant factors are. At such an early stage in the project, there may not be enough information; tailoring needs will emerge as the initiation work progresses. For this reason, it is better to start 'simple' and then elaborate if needed, rather than create a management environment suitable for a hypothetical major project.

Some projects are too complex to have a full definition of the project's output (and hence a project's final products) agreed by the end of this process. In such cases, it is common to have a project lifecycle with a number of investigative stages to look at options and choose a solution. In these cases, the initiating a project process is only used at the start of the first stage, to set up the management and control environment.

Tailoring Products within the Initiation a Project Process

The guidelines for the tailoring of the baseline management products within the Initiating a Project Process are:

PID Comprising	The PID may be a single document which includes all the components, or a set of separate documents or any combination of documents and data.
Detailed Business Case	
Risk Management Approach	
Quality Management Approach	
Change Control Approach	Change control may be known by other names in some industries/environments (e.g. asset management or parts management).
Communication Management Approach	
Project Plan	The project plan may be informal or formal, depending on the context. It may be a single document which includes the project product description, product descriptions and benefits management approach. The project plan may include components in any format commensurate with the complexity of the project, with views ranging from a simple list of accountabilities, products, activities and dates, Gantt charts or product backlog. The plan may be held totally or partially within a planning tool(s).
Project Controls	
Tailoring or Prince2 2017	

Guidelines for tailoring records management products within the Initiating a Project Process:

Risk Register	The risk register may be a part of a workbook containing issues, assumptions and decisions.
Issue Register	The issue register may be a part of a workbook containing issues, assumptions and decisions. As issues do not all result in changes, the issue register may be split into a change register (for recording and tracking change requests) and an issue register for all other issues, such as suggestions, concerns or queries. Similarly, 'off-specification' issues may also be held in a separate log.
Quality Register	The amount of information included in the quality register can vary considerably, depending on the extent to which quality metrics (e.g. 'defect counts') need to be analysed for process improvement purposes.

Tailoring the Controlling a Stage Process

The purpose of the controlling a stage process is to assign work to be done, monitor such work, deal with issues, report progress to the project board, and take corrective actions to ensure that the management stage remains within tolerance.

General considerations
The work packages are fundamentally important to this process as they relate to the PRINCE2 principle to focus on products.

Guidelines for tailoring products within the Controlling a Stage Process

Work Package	Work packages can take many forms as specialist disciplines often have their own practices for defining their specialist deliverables. They are also likely to differ if the work is done internally or contracted to a supplier.
	The project manager should use the work package outline as a checklist to ensure that the relevant content is present.
Highlight Report	The frequency of highlight reporting may change to suit the risk profile and output being created. This is documented in the communication management approach in the PID.
	Additional information, such as KPIs, may be added or referenced if it provides clarity. Highlight reports may be in the form of wall charts or Kanban boards.
Issue Report	An issue report is simply a view of the issue register with additional information covering an impact analysis, recommendation and decision. If this additional information is added to the issue register, there is no need for a separate, formally documented report.
Exception Report	As the recipients of the report are the project board members, this report may be in any format acceptable to them as long as it includes the information the project board requires.

Tailoring roles within the Controlling a Stage Process
The project manager is responsible for the creation of all new management products in this process, but may delegate this to others, while retaining accountability.

For example, PRINCE2 shows the project manager as responsible for creating work packages. However, in practice they may not have the requisite skills to define specialist products and their role is rather to see that they are defined and reviewed rigorously.

Tailoring the Managing Product Delivery Process
The purpose of the managing product delivery process is to control the link between the project manager and the team manager(s), by agreeing the requirements for acceptance, execution and delivery.
The role of the team manager(s) is to coordinate an area of work that will deliver one or more of the project's products. They can be internal or external to the customer's organization.

General Considerations
The activities in this process may be combined, split or run concurrently to suit the context, but care should be taken to ensure the integrity of the interface to the controlling a stage process.

As this process is where the specialist work is undertaken, work will be done using practices which are appropriate to the type of work. It is important that monitoring and control of specialist work is done using controls and measures which are appropriate to that work and that the project manager should incorporate them into the appropriate management products.

Work packages are not necessarily small in scale. All the PRINCE2 principles are as applicable to a work package as to a project, requiring appropriate governance and control and often needing a team manager who is skilled in project management. For large work packages, a team manager may create a hierarchy of smaller work packages to allocate to the team members. In this case the process for managing product delivery should be tailored to ensure the work in any lower-level work packages is controlled.

Tailoring roles within the Managing Product Delivery Process

Team Plan	The team plan may be a subset of the stage plan, and may be informal or formal, depending on the context.
	The team plan may include components in any format commensurate with the complexity of

	the work package, with views ranging from a simple list of accountabilities, products, activities and dates to Gantt charts. The plan may be held totally or partially within a planning tool(s).
	The team plan should be developed at the same time as the stage plan, not waiting for the work package; this will help ensure commitment and a well-integrated set of plans. In the accept a work package activity there would need to be a confirmation that the team plan is still valid.
Checkpoint Report	Checkpoint reports may be informal or formal, depending on the context. If a project manager meets with the team managers regularly, then a verbal update, captured by the project manager in a daily log to be used to create the highlight report, may be sufficient. Additional information, such as KPIs, may be added if it helps understanding of progress.

Tailoring roles within the Managing Product Delivery Process

A project manager may also undertake a team manager role.

The team manager is responsible for all activities but may be supported by team members. If a team manager is responsible for a lower-level work package, they may report to the higher-level team manager who is responsible for the next-higher-level work package.

Although the PRINCE2 processes define who creates, updates and approves a work package, these accountabilities may be changed provided both the team manager and project manager are in agreement on what the work package comprises.

Tailoring the Managing a Stage Boundary Process

The purpose of the managing a stage boundary process is to enable the project manager to provide the project board with sufficient information to be able to:

- Review the success of the current management stage
- Approve the next stage plan
- Review the updated project plan
- Confirm continued business justification and acceptability of the risks.

Therefore, the process should be executed at, or close to, the end of each management stage.

General Considerations

The activities in this process may be combined, split or run concurrently to suit the context, but care should be taken to ensure the integrity of the interfaces with the initiating a project, controlling a stage and directing a project processes.

Although this process is called managing a stage boundary, it also covers the preparation of an exception plan within a stage when tolerances are exceeded; the PRINCE2 process model may therefore be changed to separate these two functions into different processes.

Tailoring products in the Managing a Stage Boundary Process

Stage Plan	If there are only two management stages (one for initiation and the other for delivery), the stage plan can be included in the project plan.
Product descriptions	The project product description and product descriptions are key as they relate to the PRINCE2 focus on products principle. Although PRINCE2 shows the project manager as responsible for creating product descriptions, in practice they may not have the requisite skills to define specialist products. Their role may be to see that the product descriptions are defined and reviewed rigorously enough to enable planning to be undertaken confidently.
End Stage Report	If there is only one delivery stage, then the end of that stage is also the end of the project. In this case an end stage report is not needed as its content would be covered in the end project report within the closing a project process. This product may be split into two parts, one covering progress to date in detail, the other forming the basis of the decision to start the next stage.
Lessons Log	Lessons from the log or lessons report (if one has been created) may be combined with the end stage report.

Exception Plan	The plan may include components in any format commensurate with the complexity of the project, with views ranging from a simple list of accountabilities, products, activities and dates to Gantt charts. The plan may be held totally or partially within a planning tool(s).

Tailoring roles within the Managing a Stage Boundary Process

The project manager is responsible for the creation of all new management products in this process but may delegate work to others with the requisite skills, such as project support or a team manager, provided the project manager retains overall responsibility.

Tailoring the Closing a Project Process

The purpose of the closing a project process is to provide a fixed point at which acceptance of the project's product is confirmed, and to recognize that objectives set out in the original PID have been achieved (or approved changes to the objectives have been achieved), or that the project has nothing more to contribute.

General Considerations

The activities in this process may be combined, split or run concurrently to suit the context, but care should be taken to ensure the integrity of the interface to the directing a project and controlling a stage processes.

If the final stage(s) of the project includes initial operation of the outputs, the hand over products activity may not be undertaken in the project's final management stage as part of closing the project but may happen within a number of previous management stages. Closing the project would then only require confirmation that all handovers have been completed.

Tailoring roles within the Closing a Project Process

End Project Report	Any element of the composition may be provided in a separate document or information source, which should be cross-referenced. The composition may be adapted to suit the readership; for example, confidential elements, such as the review of the business case or team performance, may be included in separate documents.
Lessons Log	Lessons from the log or lessons report (if one has been created) are usually included in the end project report but may be presented in a separate document.

Prince2 2017 Foundation Study Notes
PRINCE2 FOUNDATION REVISION NOTES

Introduction

These revision notes are not designed to be your only revision, they are to provide the key points in each area that the exam questions normally focus on and are useful when focusing your revision time specifically to the exam or if you are limited with your available revision time.

The revision notes are broken-up into the following sections:

Overview and Basics (Inc. Principles)
- Themes
- Business case
- Organization
- Quality
- Plans
- Risk
- Change

Processes
- Starting up a Project (SU)

- Directing a Project (DP)
- Initiating a Project (IP)
- Controlling a Stage (CS)
- Managing Product Delivery (MP)
- Managing a Stage Boundary (SB)
- Closing a Project (CP)

Overview and Basics
Project Characteristics
- Change – A means by which we implement change
- Temporary – Defined start and End
- Cross-functional – Different skills
- Unique – Each project is unique
- Uncertain – Projects are riskier than Business as Usual (BAU)

Aspects of project performance that need to be managed, also known as objectives or variables
- Time
- Cost
- Quality
- Scope
- Benefits
- Risk

Four key elements that make up the PRINCE2 Framework
- Principles – Guidance and good/best practice
- Themes – Aspects of project management that are addressed continually throughout the project
- Processes – Lifecycle of the project
- Tailoring (environment) – Appropriate use of the framework

EXAM TIP: Principles, Themes and Processes
You will occasionally get the following question in the exam:
"Which of the following is a Principle?" or "Which of the following is NOT a Principle?"
"Which of the following is a Theme?" or "Which of the following is NOT a Theme?"
"Which of the following is a Process?" or "Which of the following is NOT a Process?"

You do NOT need to memorize all Principles, themes and processes, simply apply these 3 rules to be able to pick the right answer from a list:

Principles are statements – For example, it is: LEARN from experience, is it NOT Learning from experience

Processes start with a verb that ends "ing" – For example: Starting up a project

Themes – With the exception of the Business Case are all one word

Principles
- Continued Business Justification
- Learn from Experience
- Defined roles and responsibilities
- Manage by Stages
- Manage by Exception
- Focus on Products

- Tailor to suit the Project environment

Themes
Business Case
Purpose
Used to judge whether a project is (and remains) desirable, viable and achievable.

Basics
- Key word: "Justification"
- Owned (Responsibility of) the Executive (Marry these two together in terms of the exam

Development path
- Outline Business Case created in SU
- Detailed Business Case created in IP
- Updated during the SB process
- Reviewed when changes or issues are raised to assess impact upon the Business Case and Project Justification

Other key points
- Do Nothing should be an option included in every Business Case

Key Products
Business Case
- Documents the Justification for the project

Benefits Management Approach
- Describe how and when benefits that have actually accrued will be measures
- Created at the same time as the Detailed Business Case (IP)
- Updated at the same time (SB)
- Pass-on to Corp/Prog. management during CP process
- Owner by the Exec during the Project and the Senior User post project

Organization
Purpose
Defines and established the projects structure of accountability and responsibility.

Basics
- One person can have more than one role
- You may need more than one person to cover some roles characteristics

Details of specific roles

Project Board
- Decision making – The Directing a Project process covers the work of the Project Board

Executive
- Represents the Business Interest
- Ultimate Decision maker (Ultimately accountable for project success or failure)
- MUST be an INDIVIDUAL
- Provides funding for the project
- Owns Business Case

Senior User(s)
- Represents End users and Impacted Users
- Accountable for Benefits realisation
- Defines Customer Quality Expectations and Acceptance Criteria for the project

Senior Supplier(s)
- Represents supplier (Specialist) interests
- Accountable for the delivery of Quality
- Commits supplier (Specialist) teams or resources

Project Assurance
- Optional role but not optional responsibilities
- 3 roles (Business Assurance, User Assurance, Supplier Assurance) – they may use any term
- Checks information on behalf of a Project Board Members
- Provides guidance and advice to the Project Board members
- Provides guidance and advice to the Project Manager

Change Authority
- Approves/Rejects Requests for Change or Off-Specifications
- The Change Authority reduces the number of Requests for Change that need to go to the Project Board

Project Manager
- Reports to the Executive
- Responsible to the Day to Day management of the project
- Manages Risks and Issues that are escalated to them
- Sets-up project procedures and controls

Project Support
- Support the Project Manager (May also support the Team Manager)
- Popular activities may include: Config Management, Doc Control, Admin, maintaining of registers)
- Responsible for the Quality Register

Team Manager
- Works is covered by the Managing Product Delivery process
- Manages the work of a Work Package
- Provides progress updates in the form of Checkpoint Reports to the Project Manager

Key Products

Communication Management Approach
- Key word: HOW
- Details how (procedures, tools, techniques) we will communicate with stakeholders both INTERNAL and EXTERNAL to the project

Quality
Purpose
The means by which the project will create and verify products that are Fit for purpose.

Basics
- The right level of quality is defined as something that is **Fit for Purpose**

4 Key elements of Quality
- **Quality Planning**
  - Understanding the level of quality needed and how it will be managed
- **Quality Control**
  - Reviewing and testing
  - Quality Review Technique used
- **Quality Management Systems**
  - A set of Corporate policies and standards – External to the Project
- **Quality Assurance**
  - External to the project (The Responsibility of Corporate/Programme Management)

Quality Review Techniques
- A technique to Assess conformity of a product against its Product Description
- A technique to sign-off or Baseline a product
- This is NOT used for users to add or change a product (That would be a Request for Change)

Roles involved
- Chair – Responsible for the conduct of the review
- Administrator – Supports the chair (Minutes/actions)
- Presenter – Represents the person/team that created the product being review
- Reviewer(s) – Person or people that will review/test the product

The Chair and Reviewer roles can be combined
The Presenter and Administrator roles can be combined

Key Products

Project Product Description
A description of the final solution
- Created in Starting up a Project process
- Key headings: "Customer Quality Expectation" and "Acceptance Criteria" – provided by Senior Use

Customer Quality Expectation – Often expressed in broad terms to get a common understanding of general quality requirements

Acceptance Criteria – A specific list of measurable criteria that a project product should meet in order to be acceptable

Product Description
A description of a particular product that the project or stage needs to create

Quality Management Approach
- Key word: HOW
- Describes Procedures, tools and techniques with regards to Quality

Quality Register
- Keeps a track of the dates and results of any planned quality checks

Plans
Purpose
Defines the means for delivering products (where, how, whom, when and how much).

Levels of plans

PRINCE2 recommends different levels of plans to cater for the different levels of detail required by the different levels of Management

Recommended Levels of Plans
- Project
- Stage
- Team

NOTE: The **Team plan** is an **OPTIONAL** plan, it is therefore recommended, however, if you get asked the questions about which plans are MANDATORY, that would only be Project and Stage

NOTE: An **Exception plan** is **NOT** a level of plan, it is a replacement plan for either the Project or a Stage if one of them is in Exception and requires re-planning, once approved the Exception Plan replaces the current stage plan or project plan

A Stage Level Exception Plan is approved by the Project Board
A project Level Exception Plan must be approved by Corp, Programme or Customer

Plan Procedure
- Design the plan
- Define and analyse the products
- Identify activities and dependencies
- Prepare estimates
- Prepare the schedule
- Document the Plan
- Analyse the risks

Product Based-Planning
1. Write the Project Product Description (First step – This is a popular question)
2. Create Product Break-down Structure
3. Write Product Descriptions
4. Create Product Flow Diagram

Key Products

Product Break-down Structure (PBS)
A hierarchical breakdown of the projects products
Product Flow Diagram (PFD)
A sequence in which products need to be created

Risk
Purpose
Identify, assess and control uncertainty.

Basics
- Key word: Uncertainty (If, May, Could, Might)
- Supports the principle Continued Business Justification

Risk Appetite: An organizations unique approach to risk taking

Risk Procedure
- Identify
- Assess

- Plan
- Implement
- Communicate

Identify
- Context: The project objective that is at risk
- SU: This will go in the Daily Log and risks requiring formal management will be transferred to the Risk Register once opened in Initiating a Project Process
- IP onwards: This will go in the Risk Register

Description:
CAUSE: The Source of the risk or A known event that has brought light to a risk
EVENT: The area of uncertainty
EFFECT: The impact on the project objectives

Assess
Estimate: Assess the individual risk
- Probability: Likelihood of the risk occurring
- Impact: how it would affect objective
- Proximity: How close (in time) is the risk

Evaluate: Aggregate (Total) exposure to risk

Plan

Risk Responses - Threats	Risk Responses - Opportunities
Avoid a threat	Exploit an opportunity
Reduce a threat	Enhance an opportunity
Transfer the risk	Share the opportunity
Share the risk	Reject the opportunity
Accept the risk	
Prepare contingent plans	

Figure 17 - Prince2 2017 Risk Responses

Implement
- **Risk Owner:** Someone that will monitor and report back on an individual risk assigned to them
- **Risk Actionee:** Someone that will implement a risk response

Communicate
- Risk communication should happen throughout the management of a risk (As per stakeholder requirements in the Communication Management Approach)

Key Products

Risk Management Approach
- Key word: HOW
- Describes Procedures, tools and techniques with regards to Risk Management
- Includes an organization attitude to risk taking (Appetite – Tolerance)

- It does NOT include the Risk Budget (This is often put as an option in the answers but is WRONG)

Risk Register
- Used to keep a record and track relating to risks that are being managed within the project

Change
Purpose
Identify, assess and control and potential and approved chance to baselines.

Types of Issues
- Request for Change
- Off-Specification
- Problem/Concern

Request for change: Someone asking for something different or a proposed change to the baseline

Off-Specification: Where something has been delivered that doesn't meet the Product description (criteria or specification) asked of it, even if this is a positive it is still an off-specification

Problem or Concern: Any other issue that does not fall into the above 2 categories

Handling the Issues

Request for Change or Off-Specification: These go to the Change Authority

Problem or Concern:
– Informal issues go in the Daily Log
– Formal issues go in the Issue Register

Key Products

Issues Register
Used to record and keep track of any issue that needs to me managed
Issues Report
Provides information on an issue (Description, Impact, Options)

Daily Log
Used to capture Informal issue that do NOT need to be managed formally

Progress
Purpose
Establish mechanisms to monitor actual achievements against those planned; and control any unacceptable deviations.

Basics
- Supports the following principles:
  - Manage by exception (Popular question/answer)
  - Manage by Stages

Tolerance
A permissible deviation above or below a plan target for time and cost before the need to escalate

Exception
Where it is FORECAST that a tolerance will be exceeded

Controls
There are only 2 **Time-driven controls** in Prince2 2017:
- Highlight Report
- Checkpoint Report

Stage Boundary
A Go/No go decision point

Management Stage (This is what PRINCE2 uses)
A commitment of resources with a go/no go decision point in between
Can also be called a Delivery Stage

Technical Stage (NOT part of PRINCE2)
A piece of work that requires specific or specialist skills (although PRINCE2 recognizes technical stages and agrees that they need to be considered and included in a project, PRINCE2 does NOT include how to manage them in the framework as they are specific to a project, sector or industry)

Key Products
Highlight Report
- Progress report provided by the Project Manager (CS) to the Project Board (DP)
- These are provided at a frequency agreed as part of the Communication Management Strategy (This is a popular question/answer)

Checkpoint Report
- Progress report provide by the Team Manager (MP) to the Project Manager (CS)
- These are provided at a frequency agreed when agreeing a Work Package

End Stage Report
- Created as part of the Managing a Stage Boundary process
- Includes the Lessons Learned Report (Optional as part of the Managing a Stage Boundary Process)
- Provides confirmation on what was completed in the stage that we are coming to the end of and a progress of the project so far

End Project Report
- Provides confirmation of what was delivered by the project, along with an evaluation of the project
- Also includes: Lesson Report (This is a popular question/answer)

Processes
Starting Up a Project (SU)
Purpose
- Prevent poorly conceived projects from even being initiated
- Get the pre-requisites for Initiating a project
- Base Information

Other key information
- Classed as Pre-project
- It is triggered by the Project Mandate
- Should provide sufficient information to identify the Executive

- It's the first process in PRINCE2
- Directing a Project is the Process that follows SU (Popular question/answer)

Key Products
Project Brief
Describes the purpose, cost, time, performance requirements and constraints for the project

Directing a Project
Basics
- Process starts after Starting Up a Project (Popular question/answer)

Purpose
- To enable the Project Board to be accountable, by giving them control with key decisions, whilst also freeing up their time by delegating the day-to-day management to the Project Manager

Other key information
- Covers the work of the Project Board (Popular question/answer)
- "Provide Ad-Hoc direction" is the activity that receives Highlight reports or exception reports (This is sometimes a question/answer)

Initiating a Project
Purpose
- Set solid foundations for the project
- Understand more about what is needed to deliver the project before any significant spend in committed

Objectives
- To summarize how PRINCE2 will be tailored for the project

Key Products
- Project Initiation Documentation (PID)
- Forms the 'Contract' between the Project Manager and Project Board confirming how the project will be managed and controlled
- Forms the 'Contract' between the Project Board and Corp/Prog or Customer Organisation confirming how the project will be directed and control

Controlling a stage
Purpose
- Covers the Day-to-Day work of the Project Manager through the delivery of the project
- Focus here is on the Project Manager delivering the stages products to the right level of quality on-time and within budget by:
- Assigning work (issuing Work Packages)
- Monitoring work (Receiving Checkpoint reports and updating the Stage Plan)
- Managing risks/Issues (and escalating if needed)
- Reporting progress (Providing Highlight Reports to the Project Board)
Objective
- Focus on delivering the stages products

Managing Product Delivery
Purpose
- Provides a controlled link between the Team Manager and the Project Manager

- **Team Manager:** accepts the works, gets it done and hands it back

Managing a Stage Boundary
Basics
- Takes place towards the end of a Stage or at the Request for an Exception plan

Purpose
- Review the stage that we are coming to the end of and prepare for the next stage
- To enable the Project Board to be provided with the necessary information to approve the next stage
    - (NOTE: The approval is NOT part of this Process. The approval is part of the DP process)

Other key Points
- The Managing a Stage Boundary process is also used for the creation of an Exception Plan
- The Managing a Stage Boundary process can be triggered from the following processes:
    - Initiating a project (Towards the end of the Initiation stage)
    - Controlling a Stage (Towards the end of a management stage)
    - Directing a Project (From the request for an Exception plan)

Key products

End Stage Report
Information to be presented to the Project Board about the project performance during the stage and the project status at stage end

Stage Plan
Detailed plan for the next stage used by the Project Manager for day-2-day management of the stage

Closing a Project
Basics
Takes place towards the end of the final stage or if a premature closure to the project is requested

Purpose
Provide a fixed point for which the project solution is handed over into Business as Usual and the Project team is disbanded.

Other Key Points
- Pass-on any open risks
- Pass-on the Benefits Review Plan
- Evaluate the Project (Against v1.0 of the P.I.D and how/why it changed throughout the project)
- Archive project information (To enable future audits)

Key products
- End Project Report (Inc. Lessons Report)
- Lessons Report Defines learning points of how future project can be improved
- Draft Closure Notification (Should include final dates for costs to be charged to the project)

The PRINCE2® Foundation Examination
Sample Paper 1

Question Booklet

Multiple Choice

Exam Duration: 1-hour Instructions

1. You should attempt all 60 questions. Each question is worth one mark. 2. There is only one correct answer per question. 3. You need to answer 33 questions correctly to pass the exam. 4. Mark your answers on the answer sheet provided. Use a pencil (NOT pen). 5. You have 1 hour to complete this exam.

6. This is a 'closed book' exam. No material other than the exam paper is allowed.

Sample Paper 1 – V1.3

1) What is the first step in the recommended risk management procedure?
    a) Assess
    b) Identify
    c) Implement
    d) Plan

2) Which statements about a project's stakeholders are CORRECT?
    1) A stakeholder is anyone who thinks they will be affected by a project
    2) Stakeholders require equal amounts of engagement by the project management team
    3) Stakeholders remain unchanged throughout the project
    4) A stakeholder may be internal or external to the corporate organization
        a) 1 and 2
        b) 2 and 3
        c) 3 and 4
        d) 1 and 4

3) Identify the missing word in the following sentence. A purpose of the [?] theme is to control any unacceptable deviations from the project's objectives.
        a) change
        b) plans
        c) progress
        d) risk

4) Which is a minimum requirement for applying the organization theme?
        a) To define the project assurance role of team managers
        b) To combine roles, where possible, to simplify the organization
        c) To appoint a business change manager as senior user when the project is part of programme
        d) To define the approach to engaging with stakeholders

5) What is defined when deciding how to tailor PRINCE2 to suit the project?
        a) When the project's progress will be reviewed
        b) Which of the six tolerance areas will be included
        c) Which primary stakeholder interests will be represented
        d) When the project's outputs will be delivered

6) Which statement about the 'continued business justification' principle is CORRECT?
        a) The justification for compulsory projects does not need approval
        b) There must be no change to the reasons for a project
        c) A formal business case document is mandatory
        d) The chosen option must provide value for money

7) Which regular report provides the project board with a summary of stage status?
        a) Lessons report

b) Product status account

c) Highlight report

d) Checkpoint report

8) Which statement about the project support role is CORRECT?

a) It can be performed by the project manager

b) It is an optional role for a PRINCE2 project

c) It produces checkpoint reports for the project manager

d) It can be combined with the project assurance role

9) What must be produced, as a minimum requirement for applying the plans theme?

a) A hierarchy of all the products to be produced during a plan

b) A record of the issues that are being formally managed during a plan

c) A diagram showing the sequence of production of the planned products

d) A record of the major risks relating to the project plan

10) Which is a purpose of a project brief?

a) To capture lessons from previous projects

b) To document a common understanding of the starting point for the project

c) To confirm that the project is able to deliver the detailed business case

d) To define the quality techniques to be applied during the project

11) Which is an objective of the 'managing product delivery' process?

a) To sign off completed work packages

b) To ensure that the business case is kept under review

c) To report progress to the project board

d) To ensure that work on products is authorized

12) In which process are team plans produced?

a) Initiating a project

b) Controlling a stage

c) Managing a stage boundary

d) Managing product delivery

13) How is the 'learn from experience' principle applied?

a) By reviewing the management of previous projects

b) By defining the customer's expectations of the project's products

c) By defining cost tolerances for project objectives

d) By delegating responsibilities to a different level of management

14) Which product is a time-driven control?

a) End stage report

b) Exception report

c) Checkpoint report

d) Lessons report

15) When should the project board request a decision from corporate, programme management or customer?

a) When the stage requires resources

b) If it is forecast that project level tolerance will be exceeded

c) If the senior supplier or senior user needs to be changed

d) When any request for change needs to be approved

16) Which is a reason why the 'defined roles and responsibilities' principle must be applied?

a) Because each project will have unique outputs

b) Because more than one function may be involved in the project

c) Because projects may have duplicated or inconsistent objectives

d) Because stages provide senior management with control points

17) Which process is triggered by the project manager's request to initiate a project?

a) Starting up a project

b) Initiating a project

c) Directing a project

d) Managing a stage boundary

18) Which is an objective of the 'starting up a project' process?

a) To confirm that there are no known restrictions that would prevent the project from being delivered

b) To ensure that all team managers understand their responsibilities

c) To obtain approval for the project plan from corporate, programme management or customer

d) To prepare the project initiation documentation for authorization to initiate the project

19) Which principle is being applied when a project product description is produced?

a) Continued business justification

b) Focus on products

c) Learn from experience

d) Manage by stages

20) Which is a minimum requirement for applying the risk theme?

a) A risk breakdown structure must be created

b) A risk budget must be established for managing risks

c) Identified threats and opportunities must be documented

d) Risk checklists must be used to ensure risks are identified

1) Which statements apply to a stage plan?

. It is produced for the project during the 'initiating a project' process

. It is produced close to the time when the planned events will take place

. It provides the basis for day-to-day control by the project manager

. It provides the basis for control by the project board

a) 1 and 2

b) 2 and 3

c) 3 and 4

d) 1 and 4

2) Which is a purpose of the benefits management approach?

a) To document the justification for undertaking a project
b) To summarize project performance to date for the project board to decide what action to take next
c) To provide a schedule for measuring the achievement of benefits
d) To provide the reasons for the project, to put into the business case

23) Which is assumed to be the customer's responsibility in the PRINCE2 customer/supplier environment?
    a) To specify the desired result
    b) To provide the skills to deliver the desired result
    c) To ensure the technical integrity of a project
    d) To develop the project's products

24) Which is a purpose of the risk management approach?
    a) To define the techniques to be used when assessing project risks
    b) To summarize exposure to strategic, programme, project and operational risks
    c) To recommend responses for each of the project risks
    d) To identify suitable risk owners for each of the project risks

25) Which management product should always be updated when a product fails its quality check?
    a) Risk register
    b) Issue register
    c) Quality register
    d) Lessons log

26) Identify the missing words in the following sentence. The purpose of the [?] process is to establish solid foundations for the project.
    a) initiating a project
    b) managing product delivery
    c) directing a project
    d) managing a stage boundary

27) Which two statements about tailoring are CORRECT?
    1) Processes can be simplified or carried out in more detail.
    2) Terminology can be changed to suit organizational standards.
    3) Themes that are not relevant to the project can be excluded.
    4) Project management team members can carry out any combination of roles.
        a) 1 and 2
        b) 2 and 3
        c) 3 and 4
        d) 1 and 4

28) Which type of issue should be raised if a new product is required after a team has started work?
A. A request for change
B. An off-specification
C. A problem
D. A concern

29) Which characteristic distinguishes a project from regular business operations?

a) It produces benefits
b) It introduces business change
c) It manages stakeholders
d) It incurs cost

30) Which process is used by a team manager to coordinate work on one or more of the project's products?
   a) Initiating a project
   b) Controlling a stage
   c) Managing a stage boundary
   d) Managing product delivery

31) Who does the senior user represent when making decisions?
   a) The people or organizations that design the project's products
   b) Corporate, programme management or customer
   c) Project delivery teams
   d) The people or organizations that benefit from using the project's product

32) What is an output?
   a) Any of the project's specialist products
   b) The result of the change derived from using the project's products
   c) The measurable improvement resulting from an outcome
   d) A negative outcome

33) What is established within the 'initiating a project' process?
   a) The different ways that the project product can be delivered
   b) The formats for communicating project information to stakeholders
   c) That all of the information to develop the project brief is available
   d) That any constraints which could affect the project have been removed

34) Which roles CANNOT be combined with the role of project assurance?
.) Project manager
) Project support
) Senior user
) Executive
   a) 1 and 2
   b) 2 and 3
   c) 3 and 4
   d) 1 and 4

5) What must the project board do, as a minimum requirement for applying the change theme?
   a) Establish a change budget
   b) Request a product status account
   c) Define a change authority
   d) Agree acceptable corrective actions

6) Which statement describes a threat to a project?
   a) An uncertain event that could have a negative impact on objectives

b) An uncertain event that could have a favourable impact on objectives

c) An event that has occurred resulting in a negative impact on objectives

d) An event that has occurred resulting in a favourable impact on objectives

37) Which aspect of project performance must be managed in order to have a clear understanding of what the project is to deliver?

a) Timescale

b) Scope

c) Risk

d) Costs

38) Which is one of the four integrated elements within PRINCE2?

a) Quality

b) Role descriptions

c) Processes

d) Product descriptions

39) What should be provided by corporate, programme management or customer before the 'starting up a project' process commences?

a) A project brief with details outlining the project approach

b) Sufficient information to identify the prospective executive

c) The project initiation documentation

d) Authority to initiate a project

40) How is the 'manage by exception' principle applied?

a) By dividing the project into a minimum of two management stages

b) By setting controls to warn the higher level of management of potential problem

c) By ensuring that the project continues to be desirable, viable and achievable

d) By providing lessons so that mistakes made in previous projects do not happen

41) Which is a responsibility of the managing level within the project management team?

a) To set project-level tolerances

b) To approve the stage completion of each stage

c) To ensure that the products are produced within the constraints agreed with the project board

d) To appoint the roles in project management team

42) What is a risk cause?

a) A negative consequence of a threat occurring

b) An area of uncertainty that could create a problem

c) A positive consequence of an exploited opportunity

d) A known situation which creates uncertainty

43) Which is a purpose of the 'closing a project' process?

a) To inform the project board that the final stage is about to start

b) To provide a fixed point at which acceptance of the project product is confirmed

c) To provide the project board with sufficient information to confirm continued business justification

d) To define the handover procedures for the project's products

44) Which is a benefit of applying the 'manage by stages' principle?

a) The project management team will understand the tolerances allowed

b) The project management team will understand the customer's expectations

c) The project will have review and decision points so that progress can be assessed

d) The key stakeholders in the project will have representation on the project board

45) Which is a benefit of using PRINCE2?

a) It provides established and proven best practice and governance for project management

b) It includes techniques for critical path analysis and earned value analysis

c) It enables a project manager to be accountable for the success of a project

d) It prevents any changes after the scope of a project has been agreed

46) Which is an objective of the 'closing a project' process?

a) To check that all the project's products have been accepted by the users

b) To prepare for the final stage of the project

c) To capture the customer's quality expectations

d) To ensure that all benefits have been achieved

47) What must be used, as a minimum requirement for applying the progress theme?

a) Stage authorization

b) Highlight reporting

c) Work package authorization

d) Checkpoint reporting

48) What must be recorded in the quality management approach, as a minimum requirement for applying the quality theme?

a) The quality tools and techniques to be used

b) The project's approach to quality planning

c) The approach to managing project assurance

d) The definition of the quality records required

49) Which is a purpose of the 'directing a project' process?

a) To provide the information required to initiate a project

b) To enable overall control of a project by the project board

c) To establish the level of control required after initiation

d) To provide sufficient information to approve the next stage plan

50) Identify the missing words in the following sentence. PRINCE2 requires that the business justification is formally verified by [?] at stage boundaries.

a) corporate, programme management or customer

b) the project board

c) project support

d) the change authority

1) Which is a purpose of the organization theme?

a) To set the tolerance on the cost of resources

b) To plan the training needed for the delivery of the project
c) To define the structure of accountability and responsibilities on the project
d) To implement the controls required to manage by exception

52) Which is a purpose of the change theme?
a) To prevent changes to what was agreed in the project initiation documentation
b) To ensure any potential changes to baselined products are controlled
c) To assess and control a project's threats and opportunities
d) To identify changes needed to the project as a result of acting on lessons

53) Identify the missing word in the following sentence. Quality [?] defines the type of quality methods the project will use.
a) assurance
b) control
c) planning
d) tolerance

54) Which is a purpose of the 'starting up a project' process?
a) To ensure that the prerequisites for initiating the project are in place
b) To establish whether the project plan can meet the required target dates
c) To assemble the project initiation documentation so the project can be initiated
d) To confirm to corporate, programme management or customer that quality expectations will be met

55) Which statement about management stages is CORRECT?
a) A project can be scheduled without management stages
b) There can be more than one delivery step within a management stage
c) Several management stages can be scheduled to run at the same time
d) Delivery steps and management stages should end together

56) Which is a purpose of the quality theme?
a) To define how the project will ensure that its products are fit for purpose
b) To define the procedures for the control and modification of project products
c) To establish mechanisms to judge whether the project remains desirable and achievable
d) To enable the assessment of continuing project viability

57) Which is an objective of the 'managing a stage boundary' process?
a) To enable the project board to commit resources and expenditure required for the initiation stage
b) To review and, if necessary, update the project initiation documentation
c) To act as a break between those managing the project and those creating products
d) To ensure a periodic review is carried out to approve the products created within the completed   stage

58) Which is a task of 'defining and analysing products'?
a) Design the plan
b) Create the product flow diagram
c) Analyse the risks
d) Prepare the schedule

59) Which activity can take place within the 'managing a stage boundary' process?

a) Produce highlight reports

b) Take corrective action within stage tolerances

c) Produce an exception plan

d) Authorize a stage plan for the next stage

60) What does the 'initiating a project' process provide?

a) Information for the project board to decide if the project is aligned to business objectives

b) Approval from the project board to proceed with the project, if it is worthwhile

c) Approval from the project manager for work to be started by delivery teams

d) Definition of the suppliers' obligations for controlling the work package delivery

END OF EXAMINATION

Answers and Rationale

Question	Correct Answer	Syllabus Topic	Rationale
1	B	3.5.4	A. Incorrect. If the risk has not been identified, it cannot be assessed. 'Assess' is the second step. Ref 10.3.2, fig 10.1 B. Correct. The risk must first be identified before it can be assessed, and responses planned and then implemented. Ref 10.3.2, fig 10.1 C. Incorrect. If the risk has not been identified, it cannot be assessed. Therefore, responses cannot be planned or implemented. 'Implement' is the fourth step. Ref 10.3.2, fig 10.1 D. Incorrect. If the risk has not been identified, it cannot be assessed. Therefore, responses cannot be planned or implemented. 'Plan' is the third step. Ref 10.3.2, fig 10.1
2	D	3.2.4a	(1) Correct. There are likely to be individuals or groups who are not part of the project management team, but who may need to interact with the project or who may be affected by the project's outcome. Ref 7.1, 7.2.2, 7.3.9 (2) Incorrect. It is important to analyse who the stakeholders are and to engage with them appropriately. Ref 7.1, 7.3.9 (3) Incorrect. It is important to review and possibly update the communication management approach at each stage boundary to ensure that it still includes all the key stakeholders. Ref 7.1, 7.2.2, 7.3.9 (4) Correct. The communication management approach contains a description of the means and frequency of communication to parties both internal and external to the project. Ref 7.1, 7.2.2, 7.3.9
3	C	3.7.1a	A. Incorrect. The purpose of the change theme is to identify, assess and control any potential and approved changes to the baseline. Ref 11.1 B. Incorrect. The purpose of the plans theme is to facilitate communication and control by defining the means of delivering the products. Ref 9.1 C. Correct. A purpose of the progress theme is to provide mechanisms to monitor progress against the allowed tolerances, and the controls to escalate to the next level should any forecast suggest that one or more tolerances will be exceeded. Ref 12.1 D. Incorrect. The purpose of the risk theme is to identify, assess and control uncertainty. Ref 10.1
4	D	3.2.2	A. Incorrect. A team manager must not be assigned a project assurance role. Therefore, defining the project assurance role of team managers is not a minimum requirement for applying the organization theme. Ref 7.2, 7.3.1, 7.2.1.10 B. Incorrect. Combining roles is permissible, but not a minimum requirement for applying the organization theme. Ref 7.2, 7.2.1.1, 7.2.1.10 C. Incorrect. Within a programme environment appointing a business change manager as senior user is permissible, but not a minimum requirement for

			applying the organization theme. Ref 7.2, 7.3.3

D. Correct. To be following PRINCE2, a project must, as a minimum, define its approach to communicating and engaging with stakeholders. Ref 7.2 |
| 5 | A | 2.1g | A. Correct. The purpose of tailoring is to ensure that project controls are appropriate to the project's scale, complexity, importance, team capability and risk (e.g. the reporting and reviewing frequency and formality). Ref 3.7

B. Incorrect. The 'manage by exception' principle sets tolerances against six objectives. These six areas are not tailored. Ref 3.5, 4.3.1

C. Incorrect. The 'defined roles and responsibilities' principle defines that all three primary stakeholder interests need to be represented; business, user and supplier. These three interests are not tailored. Ref 3.3, 4.3.1

D. Incorrect. In PRINCE2, projects deliver outputs in the form of products. Tailoring is not on the specialist products but on the project management method and project controls. Ref 3.7, 6.1 |
| 6 | D | 2.1a | A. Incorrect. The business justification for a project, compulsory or not, must be documented and approved. Ref 3.1

B. Incorrect. Although the justification should remain valid, it may change. Ref 3.1

C. Incorrect. The format and formality of documentation may vary depending on need and circumstance. Ref 3.1

D. Correct. Even compulsory projects should be supported by business justification, even if only to demonstrate that the chosen option represents value for money. Ref 3.1 |
| 7 | C | 3.7.1b | A. Incorrect. The lessons report is used to pass on any lessons that can be usefully applied to other projects. Ref 19.4.4, A.15.1

B. Incorrect. The purpose of the product status account is to provide information about the state of the products within defined limits. Ref 11.1, A.18.1

C. Correct. A highlight report is used to provide the project board with a summary of the stage status at intervals it has defined. The project board uses the report to monitor stage and project progress. Ref 12.2.2.4, A.11.1

D. Incorrect. A checkpoint report is used by a team manager to report the status of a work package to the project manager. Ref 12.2.2.4, A.4.1 |
| 8 | A | 3.2.3i | A. Correct. The project manager performs the project support role unless this is delegated to another person/other people. Ref 7.2.1.9

B. Incorrect. The project support role is not an optional role for a PRINCE2 project. It must either be performed by the project manager or be delegated by the project manager. Ref 7.2.1.9

C. Incorrect. The team manager produces checkpoint reports, not project support. Ref 7.2.1.8, 7.2.1.9, tab 12.2 |

			D. Incorrect. Project support cannot be combined with the project assurance role. The two roles should be separate in order to maintain the independence of project assurance. Ref 7.2.1.10
9	A	3.4.2	A. Correct. PRINCE2 requires that three products are produced and maintained. This includes the product breakdown structure: a hierarchy of all the products to be produced during a plan. Ref 9.2 B. Incorrect. It is the issue register that captures and maintains information issues that are being managed formally. It is not a minimum requirement for applying the plans theme. Ref 9.2, 11.4.1 C. Incorrect. It is the product flow diagram that provides a diagram showing the sequence of production and interdependencies of the planned products. Product flow diagrams are recommended but not required. Ref 9.2, 9.3.1.2 D. Incorrect. It is the risk register which provides record of identified risks relating to the plan, including their status and history. It is not a minimum requirement for applying the plans theme. Ref 9.2, 10.2
10	B	4.1h	A. Incorrect. It is the purpose of the lessons log to capture lessons from previous projects. Ref A.14.1 B. Correct. An agreed project brief ensures that the project has a commonly understood and well-defined start point. Ref A.19.1, 14.4.5 C. Incorrect. The detailed business case is produced in the 'initiating a project' process and the project brief is produced earlier in the 'starting up a project' process. Ref 16.4.8, 14.4.5 D. Incorrect. A quality management approach is used to define the quality techniques and standards to be applied, and the various responsibilities for achieving the required quality levels during the project. Ref A.22.1
11	D	4.2e	A. Incorrect. Completed work packages are signed-off in the 'controlling a stage' process. Ref 17.4 B. Incorrect. It is an objective of the 'controlling a stage' process is to ensure that the business case is kept under review. The business case is not reviewed within the 'managing product delivery' process. Ref 17.2, 18.2 C. Incorrect. Progress is reported to the project board by the project manager, via highlight reports, within the 'controlling a stage' process. The team manager would report progress to the project manager, via checkpoint reports, within the 'managing product delivery' process. Ref 17.4, 18.2 D. Correct. It is an objective of the 'managing product delivery' process to ensure that work on products allocated to the team is authorized and agreed. Ref 18.2
12	D	4.3e	A. Incorrect. Team plans are not produced by the team manager during the 'initiating a project' process. Ref 18.3 B. Incorrect. Team plans are not produced by the team manager during the 'controlling a stage' process. Ref 18.3

			C. Incorrect. Team plans are not produced by the team manager during the 'managing a stage boundary' process. Ref 18.3
			D. Correct. Team plans are produced by the team manager during the 'managing product delivery' process. Ref 18.3
13	A	2.1b	A. Correct. When starting a project, previous or similar projects should be reviewed to see if lessons could be applied. Ref 3.2
			B. Incorrect. A PRINCE2 project applies the principle 'focus on products'. It focuses on the definition and delivery of products, in particular the quality requirements. Ref 3.6
			C. Incorrect. A PRINCE2 project applies the principle 'manage by exception'. It has defined tolerances for project objectives, in order to establish limits of delegated authority. Ref 3.5
			D. Incorrect. A PRINCE2 project applies the principle 'manage by stages' principle. The project board delegates the authority for day-to-day control of a management stage, within agreed tolerances, to the project manager. Ref 3.4
14	C	3.7.3a	A. Incorrect. The end of a stage is not a time-driven (periodic) control. For example, it does not occur weekly or monthly. Ref 12.2.2
			B. Incorrect. Exception situations are not a time-driven (periodic) control. You cannot plan for them. Ref 12.2.2
			C. Correct. Time-driven controls take place at predefined periodic intervals. The frequency and format of the checkpoint reports will be agreed in the work package. Ref 12.2.2
			D. Incorrect. Lessons reports are usually produced at the end of a stage and the end of the project. These are not time-driven (periodic) controls, for example they are not produced monthly, or weekly. Ref 12.2.2, 12.2.2.3
15	B	3.7.3b	A. Incorrect. It is a project board responsibility to approve resources for the stage. Ref tab 7.1
			B. Correct. The project board should refer to corporate, programme management or customer if project level tolerance is forecast to be exceeded because this tolerance is set by corporate, programme management or customer. Ref 12.2.1
			C. Incorrect. The executive is responsible for a change in senior user or supplier. This does not require higher level approval. Ref tab 7.1
			D. Incorrect. Approval of a request for change is normally handled by the project board or the change authority. It would only be referred to corporate, programme management or customer if project tolerances would be exceeded. Ref 11.2, tab 11.2
16	B	2.1c	A. Incorrect. The fact that projects have unique outputs is a reason for the 'focus on products' principle. Ref 3.6
			B. Correct. A project is typically cross-functional and agreeing roles and responsibilities ensures that the people involved know what's expected of

			them and what to expect of others. Ref 3.3 C. Incorrect. The need to avoid duplicated or inconsistent objectives is a reason for the 'continued business justification' principle. Ref 3.1. D. Incorrect. The need for control points is a reason for the 'manage by stages' principle. Ref 3.4
17	C	4.3b	A. Incorrect. The 'starting up a project' process prepares for the authorization of the initiation stage. The request to initiate the project is an action carried out during the 'starting up a project' process. Ref 14.1 B. Incorrect. The 'initiating a project' process prepares documentation to be submitted to the project board for project authorization, but the actual authorization comes from the 'directing a project' process. Ref 16.3 C. Correct. Only the project board can authorize project initiation, and its activities are covered in the 'directing a project' process. Ref 15.3 D. Incorrect. The 'managing a stage boundary' process prepares information, in order to request authorization of the next stage from the project board. Ref 19.1
18	A	4.2a	A. Correct. An objective of the 'starting up a project' process is to ensure time is not wasted on initiating any projects that are based on unsound assumptions. Ref 14.2 B. Incorrect. The project management team is designed during the 'starting up a project' process, but the actual team managers may not be appointed until the 'managing a stage boundary' process. Ref 14.4.3 C. Incorrect. The project plan is created in the 'initiating a project' process and approved by the project board in the 'directing a project' process. Ref 16.4.7, 15.4.2 D. Incorrect. The project initiation documentation is prepared in the 'initiating a project' process. Ref 16.4.9
19	B	2.1f	A. Incorrect. The 'continued business justification' principle is applied through regular planned reviews of the business case during the life of the project to confirm its continued viability. Ref 3.1 B. Correct. Producing the project product description applies the 'focus on products' principle by clearly defining the project's product, the customer's quality expectations and acceptance criteria. Ref 3.6 / A.21.1 C. Incorrect. The 'learn from experience' principle is applied to ensure that project teams learn from previous experience: lessons are sought, recorded and acted upon throughout the life of the project. Ref 3.2 D. Incorrect. Applying the 'manage by stages' principle enables the extent of senior management control over projects to be varied according to the business priority, risk and complexity involved. Ref 3.4
20	C	3.5.2	A. Incorrect. A risk breakdown structure is a risk management technique. It is not a minimum requirement for applying the risk theme. Ref 10.4.1.2, 10.2

			B. Incorrect. It might be appropriate to identify an explicit risk budget within the project budget; however, this is not a minimum requirement for applying the risk theme. Ref 10.3.7, 10.2 C. Correct. PRINCE2 requires that a risk register is used to capture all identified threats and opportunities. Ref. 10.2 D. Incorrect. A risk checklist is a risk management technique. It is not a minimum requirement for applying the risk theme. Ref 10.4.1.2, 10.2
21	B	3.4.1b	(1) Incorrect. A stage plan is required for each management stage, not for the whole project. Ref 9.2.1.2 (2) Correct. A stage plan is created towards the end of the preceding stage as part of the 'managing a stage boundary' process. It is produced close to the time when the planned events will take place. Ref 9.2.1.2 (3) Correct. A stage plan is created at the level of detail needed to enable the day-to-day control by the project manager. Ref 9.2.1.2 (4) Incorrect. The stage plan provides the basis for the project manager's control. The project board monitors against the project plan. Ref 9.2.1.2, 9.2.1.1
22	C	3.1.1b	A. Incorrect. This is a purpose of the business case. Ref A.2.1 B. Incorrect. This is the purpose of the end stage report. Ref A.9.1 C. Correct. The benefits management approach is used to cover the assessment of benefits. Ref 6.2.2 / A.1.1 D. Incorrect. The reasons for the project are derived from the project mandate and documented in the outline business case during the 'starting up a project' process. Ref 14.4.4
23	A	1.2b	A. Correct. It is assumed that there will be a customer who will specify the desired result and probably pay for the project. Ref 4.3.4.3 B. Incorrect. It is assumed that the suppliers will provide the resources and skills to deliver the desired result, not the customer. Ref 4.3.4.3 C. Incorrect. This is a supplier responsibility, not the responsibility of the customer. Ref 7.2.1.4 D. Incorrect. This is a supplier responsibility, not the responsibility of the customer. Ref 7.2.1.4

24	A	3.5.1b	A. Correct. The risk management approach describes the specific risk management techniques and standards to be applied, and the responsibilities for achieving an effective risk management procedure. Ref A.24.1
			B. Incorrect. Exposure to risk is summarized in the risk profile. This procedure is defined in the risk management approach. Ref A.24.2
			C. Incorrect. The risk management approach defines the different categories of risk responses which can be used to identify suitable actions for each risk. It does not define the specific response actions appropriate for each risk. Ref A.24.2
			D. Incorrect. Risk owners are identified and recorded in the risk register. Ref A.25.2
25	C	3.3.1b	A. Incorrect. This event has already happened. There is no uncertainty about its occurrence, therefore it is not a risk. Ref 10.1 / A.25.1
			B. Incorrect. This may be raised as an issue (off-specification) and formally managed if, for example, the failure is likely to lead to an exception situation. However, the product that should always be updated with the result of the quality activities is the quality register. Ref 8.2, A.23.1
			C. Correct. The quality register records the results of all quality management activities. Ref 8.2, A.23.1
			D. Incorrect. There may be lessons to be learned, but this is not always the case. The product that should always be updated with the result of the quality activities is the quality register. Ref 8.2, 12.2.2.3, A14.1, A.23.1
26	A	4.1c	A. Correct. The purpose of the 'initiating a project' process is to establish solid foundations for the project, enabling the organization to understand the work that needs to be done to deliver the project's products before committing to a significant spend. Ref 16.1
			B. Incorrect. The purpose of the 'managing product delivery' process is to control the link between the project manager and team manager(s). Ref 18.1
			C. Incorrect. The purpose of the 'directing a project' process is to enable the project board to be accountable for the project's success. The project board does this by making key decisions and exercising overall control while delegating day-to-day management of the project to the project manager. Ref 15.1
			D. Incorrect. The purpose of the 'managing a stage boundary' process is to enable the project board to be provided with sufficient information by the project manager so that it can review the success of the current stage, approve the next stage plan, review the updated project plan, and confirm continued business justification and acceptability of the risks. Ref 19.1
27	A	2.2	(1) Correct. Processes can be combined or adapted. Ref. 4.3.1.

			(2) Correct. Terminology can be changed to suit other standards or policies. Ref. 4.3.1
			(3) Incorrect. All the themes must be applied in a project; however, they should be tailored according to the complexity of the project. Ref 5.1
			(4) Incorrect. Some project roles cannot be shared or combined, such as the project manager and the executive. Ref. 7.2.1.10
28	A	3.6.3a	A. Correct. The product description should have been baselined before work began. Therefore, this is a request for change to a baselined product. Ref tab 11.1
			B. Incorrect. An off-specification is something that should be provided by the project, but currently is not (or is forecast not to be). It might be a missing product or a product not meeting its specifications. Ref tab 11.1
			C. Incorrect. A problem, or concern, is a type of issue (other than a request for change or off-specification) that the project manager needs to resolve or escalate. Ref tab 11.1
			D. Incorrect. A concern, or problem, is a type of issue (other than a request for change or off-specification) that the project manager needs to resolve or escalate. Ref tab 11.1
29	B	1.1a	A. Incorrect. Both projects and business as usual may produce benefits. This is not one of the characteristics that make projects different. Ref 2.1
			B. Correct. Projects are the means by which we introduce business change. When the change is implemented, business as usual resumes (in its new form). Ref 2.1
			C. Incorrect. Both projects and business as usual involve managing stakeholders. This is not one of the characteristics that make projects different. Ref 2.1
			D. Incorrect. Both projects and business as usual incur costs. This is not one of the characteristics that make projects different. Ref 2.1
30	D	4.1e	A. Incorrect. The purpose of the 'initiating a project' process is to enable the organization to understand the work that needs to be done to deliver the project's products before committing to a significant spend. The 'managing product delivery' process enables the team manager(s) is to coordinate an area of work that will deliver one or more of the project's products. Ref 16.1, 18.1
			B. Incorrect. The purpose of the 'controlling a stage' process is to assign work to be done. The 'managing product delivery' process enables the team manager(s) to coordinate an area of work that will deliver one or more of the project's products. Ref 17.1, 18.1
			C. Incorrect. The purpose of the 'managing a stage boundary' process is to plan the work of the next stage. The 'managing product delivery' process enables the team manager(s) is to coordinate an area of work that will

			deliver one or more of the project's products. Ref 19.1, 18.1
			D. Correct. The 'managing product delivery' process enables the team manager(s) to coordinate an area of work that will deliver one or more of the project's products. Ref 18.1
31	D	3.2.3c	A. Incorrect. The senior supplier represents the designers of the project's products. Ref 7.2.1.4
			B. Incorrect. The senior user is appointed by the executive to represent the user needs and does not make decisions on behalf of corporate management. Ref 7.2.1.3
			C. Incorrect. The senior supplier represents the project development teams. Ref 7.2.1.4
			D. Correct. The senior user makes decisions on behalf of those who will benefit from the use of the project's products. Ref 7.2.1.3
32	A	3.1.3	A. Correct. This is an output - a specialist product that is handed over to a user (or users). Note that management products are not outputs but are created solely for the purpose of managing the project. Ref glossary, 6.1
			B. Incorrect. This is an outcome - the result of change, normally affecting real-world behaviour and/or circumstances. Outcomes are desired when a change is conceived. They are achieved as a result of the activities undertaken to effect the change. Ref glossary, 6.1
			C. Incorrect. This is a benefit - the measurable improvement resulting from an outcome perceived as an advantage by one or more stakeholders. Ref glossary, 6.1
			D. Incorrect. This is a dis-benefit - a measurable decline resulting from an outcome perceived as negative by one or more stakeholders, which reduces one or more organizational objective(s). Ref glossary, 6.1
33	B	4.2c	A. Incorrect. The available project approaches are evaluated in the 'starting up a project' process. Ref 14.2 / 14.4.5
			B. Correct. An objective of the 'initiating a project' process is to ensure that there is common understanding of who needs information, in what format, and at what time. Ref 16.2 / 16.4.5
			C. Incorrect. The project brief is developed in the 'starting up a project' process not the 'initiating a project' process. Ref 14.2
			D. Incorrect. A focus of the 'initiating a project' process is to understand and put strategies in place to manage constraints, not to remove them. Ref 16.2
34	A	3.2.3e	(1) Correct. Project assurance must be independent of the project manager. Ref 7.2.1.10, tab 6.1
			(2) Correct. Project assurance must be independent of project support. Ref 7.2.1.10, tab 7.1

			(3) Incorrect. Project assurance is a responsibility of the project board. The senior user is a member of the project board. Ref 7.2.1.3, tab 6.1 (4) Incorrect. Project assurance is a responsibility of the project board. The executive is a member of the project board. Ref 7.2.1.2, fig 5.4 tab 7.1
35	C	3.6.2	A. Incorrect. Unless the anticipated level of change on a project is low, it is advisable for a budget to be set up to pay for changes, but this is not a minimum requirement for applying the change theme. Ref 11.2, 11.3.6 B. Incorrect. When reviewing management stage status, a product status account can be requested. However, this is not a minimum requirement for applying the change theme. Ref 17.4.4, 11.2 C. Correct. To be following PRINCE2, a project must, as a minimum, define the roles and responsibilities for change control, including a defined change authority. Ref 11.2 D. Incorrect. There is no minimum requirement to agree acceptable corrective actions. Ref 11.2
36	A	3.5.3a	A. Correct. A threat may have a negative impact on the project objectives. Ref 10.1 B. Incorrect. Events that may have favourable impacts on objectives are opportunities, not threats. Ref 10.1 C. Incorrect. Threats are future uncertain events, not something that has already occurred; these events are called issues. Ref 10.1, 11.1 D. Incorrect. Threats are future uncertain events, not something that has already occurred; these events are called issues. Ref 10.1, 11.1
37	B	1.1b	A. Incorrect. Failure to deliver on time may affect what products can be delivered but does not affect the understanding of what the project is to deliver. Ref 2.3 B. Correct. Clear agreement on scope will avoid users and suppliers making incorrect assumptions about what is to be delivered. Ref 2.3 C. Incorrect. Risk is one of the six aspects but does not affect understanding of the deliverables required. Ref 2.3 D. Incorrect. Project costs need to be managed to avoid overspending, but this will not clarify understanding of what the project is to deliver. Ref 2.3
38	C	1.1d	A. Incorrect. Quality is an aspect of project performance that needs to be managed. The integrated elements are the principles, themes, processes and the project environment. Ref 1.1 B. Incorrect. Role descriptions help to agree and communicate project management team roles and responsibilities. The integrated elements are the principles, themes, processes and the project environment. Ref 1.1

			C. Correct. The integrated elements are the principles, themes, processes and the project environment. Ref 1.1
			D. Incorrect. Product descriptions support the focus on products, but the integrated elements are the principles, themes, processes and the project environment. Ref 1.1
39	C	4.3a	A. Incorrect. The project mandate is refined to produce a project brief. Corporate, programme management or customer provides a project mandate, but the assembly of a project brief is the responsibility of the project management team. Ref 16.4.9
			B. Correct. The project mandate, provided by corporate, programme management or customer, should include sufficient information to identify at least the prospective executive of the project board. Ref 14.3
			C. Incorrect. The project initiation documentation is developed by the project management team during the 'initiating a project' process. Ref 16.4.9
			D. Incorrect. The project board provides the authority to initiate a project after it has reviewed and is satisfied with the outputs from the 'starting up a project' process. Ref 15.4.1
40	B	2.1e	A. Incorrect. To apply the 'manage by stages' principle, a project must have at least two management stages. Ref 3.4
			B. Correct. Accountability is established by setting up controls so that if tolerances are forecast to be exceeded, the next higher management layer can be consulted and decide how to proceed. Ref 3.4
			C. Incorrect. By applying the 'continued business justification' principle, project management can ensure that the project is desirable, viable and achievable. Ref 3.1
			D. Incorrect. By applying the 'learn from experience' principle, lessons can be found that can be applied in the project. Ref 3.2
41	C	3.2.3g	A. Incorrect. This is a corporate level responsibility. Ref 7.1, fig 7.2
			B. Incorrect. This is a project board (directing level) responsibility and not a managing (project manager) responsibility. Ref 7.1, fig 7.2
			C. Correct. The managing layer of the project is the project manager and the project manager have to ensure that the project produces the required products in accordance with the tolerance levels set by the project board. Ref 7.1, fig 7.2
			D. Incorrect. This is an executive (directing level) responsibility. Ref 7.1, fig 7.2
42	D	3.5.3d	A. Incorrect. This is describing a risk effect. The risk effect is the impact(s) that the risk would have on the project objectives if the risk materializes. Ref 10.4.1.2
			B. Incorrect. This is describing a risk event. The risk event is the area of

			uncertainty in terms of the threat or the opportunity. Ref 10.4.1.2
			C. Incorrect. This is describing a risk effect. The risk effect is the impact(s) that the risk would have on the project objectives if the risk materializes. Ref 10.4.1.2
			D. Correct. This is describing a risk cause. The risk cause should describe the source of the risk, i.e. the situation that gives rise to the risk. These are often referred to as risk drivers. Ref 10.4.1.2
43	B	4.1g	A. Incorrect. The 'closing a project' process is carried out within the final stage of the project. The notification to the project board that the final (or any) stage is about to start comes from the 'managing a stage boundary' process. Ref 19.4
			B. Correct. A purpose of the 'closing a project' process is to provide a fixed point at which acceptance of the project product is confirmed. Ref 20.1
			C. Incorrect. A purpose of the 'managing a stage boundary' process is to provide the project board with sufficient information to confirm continued business justification for the project. Ref 19.1
			D. Incorrect. The handover procedures for the project's products are defined in the 'initiating a project' process as part of defining the change control approach. Ref 11.2, A.3
44	C	2.1d	A. Incorrect. Understanding delegated authority and established tolerances is a benefit of applying the 'manage by exception' principle. Ref 3.5
			B. Incorrect. Understanding the customer's expectations and acceptance criteria is a benefit of applying the 'focus on products' principle. Ref 3.6
			C. Correct. The 'manage by stages' principle provides review and decision points, so the project board can assess the viability of the project. Ref 3.4
			D. Incorrect. The business, user and supplier stakeholders being represented on the project is a benefit of applying the 'defined roles and responsibilities' principle. Ref 3.3
45	A	1.2a	A. Correct. PRINCE2 is based on established and proven best practice and governance for project management. Ref 1
			B. Incorrect. There are many proven planning and control techniques that can be used in support of the PRINCE2 themes, for example, critical path analysis (in planning) and earned value analysis (in progress control). Some techniques are described within the guidance, however alternative, equivalent techniques can be substituted, provided they meet the minimum requirements for applying the theme. Ref 1.2
			C. Incorrect. Whilst it is a benefit to have a single person accountable for a project, in the case of PRINCE2, this person is the executive, not a project manager. Ref 7.2.1.2
			D. Incorrect. Projects are all about change, even after the products have

			been baselined. 2.1
46	A	4.2g	A. Correct. A purpose of the 'closing a project' process is to verify user acceptance of a project's products. Ref 20.2 B. Incorrect. The 'closing a project' process occurs during the final stage, which is prepared during the 'managing a stage boundary' process, as is any other stage, except for the initiation stage. Ref 20.3 C. Incorrect. The customer's quality expectations are defined and agreed early in the 'starting up a project' process. The expectations are captured in discussions with the customer (business and user stakeholders) and then refined for inclusion in the project product description. Ref 14.4.4 D. Incorrect. It is likely that not all benefits will be achieved before the project closes. Some will be measured post-project as part of a benefits review. Ref 20.4.3
47	A	3.7.2	A. Correct. To be following PRINCE2, a project must, as a minimum, be managed by stages (PRINCE2's 'manage by stages' principle). Ref 12.2 B. Incorrect. There are no reports specified in the minimum requirements for applying the progress theme. Ref 12.2 C. Incorrect. Authorization of work packages is not specified as a minimum requirement for applying the progress theme. Ref 12.2 D. Incorrect. There are no reports specified in the minimum requirements for applying the progress theme. Ref 12.2
48	C	3.3.2	A. Incorrect. The particular quality tools and techniques to be used do not need to be defined as a minimum requirement for applying the quality theme, although the overall approach to quality control must be defined. Ref 8.2 B. Incorrect. The project's approach to quality planning does not need to be defined as a minimum requirement for applying the quality theme, although the overall approach to quality control must be defined. Ref 8.2 C. Correct. To be following PRINCE2, a project must, as a minimum, define its quality management approach. This approach must minimally cover: the project's approach to quality control; the project's approach to project assurance; how the management of quality is communicated throughout the project lifecycle; and the roles and responsibilities for quality management. Ref 8.2. D. Incorrect. The quality records to be used do not have to be defined as a minimum requirement for applying the quality theme. However, the approach to quality control, how quality is communicated, and the roles/responsibilities related to managing quality must be defined. Ref 8.2
49	B	4.1b	A. Incorrect. A purpose of the 'starting up a project' process is to provide the information required to confirm whether it is worthwhile to initiate a project. Ref 14.1 B. Correct. A purpose of the 'directing a project' process is to establish

			the level of control required by the project board after initiation. Ref 15.1
			C. Incorrect. The project controls are set up during the 'initiating a project' process. Ref 16.4.6
			D. Incorrect. A purpose of the 'managing a stage boundary' process is to provide sufficient information to review the current stage and approve the next stage plan. Ref 19.1
50	B	3.1.2	A. Incorrect. Corporate, programme management or customer sets the overall requirements and tolerance levels for the project but is not directly involved in its management. It is the project board that formally verifies the business justification at stage boundaries and only refers to corporate, programme management or the customer if the project is no longer justified. Ref 7.2, 12.2.4
			B. Correct. In PRINCE2, the business justification is developed at the beginning of the project and reviewed and updated throughout the life of the project. It is formally verified by the project board at each key decision point, such as at stage boundaries, and is confirmed throughout the period that the benefits are realized. Ref 6.2
			C. Incorrect. Project support advises on events that may impact the business case but does not formally verify it at stage boundaries. Ref tab 6.1
			D. Incorrect. The project board may delegate the authority to approve responses to requests for change or off-specifications to a separate individual or group, called a change authority. They cannot delegate their responsibility for verifying the business justification at stage boundaries. Ref 7.2.1.6, 6.2
51	C	3.2.1a	A. Incorrect. The setting of tolerances is part of the progress theme. Ref 12.1
			B. Incorrect. The purpose of the plans theme is to plans how the products will be achieved and by whom and to estimate timescales and cost. Ref 9.1, 9.1.1.
			C. Correct. The purpose of the organization theme is to define and establish the project's structure of accountability and responsibilities (the who?). Ref 7.1
			D. Incorrect. To apply the principle 'manage by exception', targets and tolerances must be set against the six aspects of project performance to be managed. This is part of the application of the progress theme. Ref 12.1
52	B	3.6.1a	A. Incorrect. Change is not prevented, it is controlled. Ref 11.1
			B. Correct. The aim of change control is not to prevent change, it is to ensure that every change is agreed by the relevant authority before it takes place. Ref 11.1
			C. Incorrect. This is a purpose of the risk theme, which is to identify,

			assess and control uncertainty and, thus, improve the ability of the project to succeed. Ref 11.1, 10.1, 10.4.1.2 D. Incorrect. It is a purpose of the quality theme to implement continuous improvement during the project by capturing and learning lessons. Ref 8.2
53	C	3.3.3a	A. Incorrect. Quality assurance may define the type of quality methods the corporate organization uses, as part of the quality management system, but quality assurance is independent from the project. It is a project responsibility, as part of quality planning, to define the type of quality methods the project will use and include this in the project's quality management approach, (although this may refer back to the corporate organization's quality management system). Ref 8.3.5, 8.1.1 B. Incorrect. Quality planning, not quality control, defines the type of quality methods the project will use. This information is included in the project's quality management approach. Ref 8.1.1 C. Correct. It is a project responsibility, as part of quality planning, to define the type of quality methods the project will use and include this in the project's quality management approach, (although this may refer back to the corporate organization's quality management system). Ref 8.1.1 D. Incorrect. Quality planning defines the type of quality methods the project will use. This information is included in the project's quality management approach. Quality tolerances are defined as part of quality planning. Ref 8.1.1
54	A	4.1a	A. Correct. The purpose of the 'starting up a project' process is to ensure that the question "do we have a viable and worthwhile project?" can be answered. This is achieved by ensuring that the prerequisites for initiating the project are in place. Ref 14.1 B. Incorrect. The project plan is assembled in the 'initiating a project' process not the 'starting up a project' process. Ref 16.4.7 C. Incorrect. The project initiation documentation is created in the 'initiating a project' process not the 'starting up a project' process. Ref 16.4.9 D. Incorrect. The customer's quality expectations are captured and documented in the project product description during the 'starting up a project' process. There is no confirmation that these will be met at this point in time as they are a target objective. Ref 14.4.4
55	B	3.4.3c	A. Incorrect. PRINCE2 mandates at least two management stages; an initiation stage and at least one further management stage. Ref 9.2 B. Correct. There may be more than one delivery step per management stage. Ref 9.3.1.1 C. Incorrect. Delivery steps often overlap but management stages do not. Management stages equate to commitment of resources and authority to

			spend. Ref 9.3.1.1 D. Incorrect. The end of a management stage does not necessarily need to occur at the same time as the end of a delivery step. Ref 9.3.1.1
56	A	3.3.1a	A. Correct. The quality theme defines the PRINCE2 approach to ensuring that the project's products meet business expectations. Ref 8.1 B. Incorrect. This is covered by the change theme. The purpose of the change theme is to identify, assess and control any potential and approved changes to the project baselines. Ref 11.1 C. Incorrect. This is covered by the business case theme. The purpose of the business case theme is to establish mechanisms to judge whether the project is (and remains) desirable, viable and achievable. Ref 6.1 D. Incorrect. This is a purpose of the progress theme. The purpose of the progress theme is to establish mechanisms to monitor and compare actual achievements against those planned, to provide a forecast for the project objectives and the project's continued viability and control any unacceptable deviations. Ref 12.1
57	B	4.2f	A. Incorrect. Commencement of the initiation stage is approved by the project board during the 'directing a project' process, at the end of start-up. This is not a stage boundary. Ref 15.4.1 B. Correct. Reviewing and, if necessary, updating the project initiation documentation (in particular the business case, project plan, project approach, strategies, project management team structure and role descriptions) is an objective of the 'managing a stage boundary' process. Ref 19.2 C. Incorrect. It is the 'managing product delivery' process that controls the link between the project manager and the teams delivering the products. Ref 18.1 D. Incorrect. Products are assessed and approved when they are completed, during the 'managing product delivery' process. These quality checks are not left until the end of the stage. Ref 18.4.2
58	B	3.4.3b	A. Incorrect. This is the first step in the planning procedure and is a prerequisite for planning. It is not part of 'defining and analysing products'. Ref 9.3.1.2 B. Correct. This is a task of 'defining and analysing products'. Ref 9.3.1.2 C. Incorrect. This is a step in the planning procedure and it is not part of 'defining and analysing products'. Ref 9.3.1.2 D. Incorrect. This is a step in the planning procedure and it is not part of 'defining and analysing products'. Ref 9.3.1.2
59	C	4.3f	A. Incorrect. Highlight reports are produced within the 'controlling a stage' process. Ref 17.4.5, 17.3, fig 17.1

			B. Incorrect. The project manager can take corrective action provided the action does not exceed any of the stage tolerances, or unless authority has been given by the project board. However, this is done within the 'controlling a stage' process. Ref 17.3, fig 17.1

C. Correct. In response to an exception report, the project board may request that the current stage (and possibly the project) is replanned. The output from re-planning is an exception plan which is produced within the 'managing a stage boundary' process. Ref 19.3, fig 19.1, 19.4.5, 9.2.1.3

D. Incorrect. Stage plans are authorized by the project board within the 'directing a project' process. Ref 15.4.3 |
| 60 | A | 4.3c | A. Correct. The 'initiating a project' process enables the project board to decide whether the project is aligned to customer objectives. Ref. 16.3

B. Incorrect. The 'directing a project' process, not the 'initiating a project' process, gives the project board the authority to approve the project. Ref. 15.3

C. Incorrect. The 'controlling a stage' process, not the 'initiating a project' process, gives the project manager the authority to approve the work to be done by the teams. Ref. 17.3

D. Incorrect. The 'controlling a stage' process, not the 'initiating a project' process, defines the suppliers' obligations for the delivery of the work package. Ref. 17.3 |

Made in the USA
Lexington, KY
28 February 2018